20TH CENTURY AMERICAN
SHORT STORIES
REVISED EDITION
VOLUME 2

Jean A. McConochie
Pace University, New York

Heinle & Heinle Publishers

I(T)P An International Thomson Publishing Company

Pacific Grove • Albany • Bonn • Boston • Cincinnati • Detroit • London • Madrid • Melbourne • Mexico City
New York • Paris • San Francisco • Tokyo • Toronto • Washington

Heinle & Heinle Publishers
20 Park Plaza
Boston, MA 02116 U.S.A.

International Thomson
Publishing
Berkshire House 168–173
High Holborn
London WC1V7AA
England

Thomas Nelson Australia
102 Dodds Street
South Melbourne, 3205
Victoria, Australia

Nelson Canada
1120 Birchmont Road
Scarborough, Ontario
Canada M1K5G4

International Thomson
Publishing Gmbh
Königwinterer Strasse 418
53227 Bonn
Germany

International Thomson
Publishing Asia
Block 221 Henderson Road
#08–03
Henderson Industrial Park
Singapore 0315

International Thomson
Publishing—Japan
Hirakawacho-cho Kyowa
Building, 3F
2-2-1 Hirakawacho-cho
Chiyoda-ku, 102 Tokyo
Japan

The publication of *Twentieth Century American Short Stories*, Volume II was directed by the members of the Newbury House Publishing Team at Heinle & Heinle:

Erik Gundersen, Editorial Director
John F. McHugh, Market Development Director
Kristin Thalheimer, Production Services Coordinator
Elizabeth Holthaus, Director of Production and Team Leader
Amy Lawler, Managing Developmental Editor

Also participating in the publication of this program:

Publisher: Stanley J. Galek
Project Manager: Margaret Cleveland
Assistant Editor: Karen P. Hazar
Associate Production Editor: Maryellen Eschmann
Manufacturing Coordinator: Mary Beth Hennebury
Interior Designer: Winston • Ford Design
Compositor: Pre-Press Company, Inc.
Cover and interior photos: Jon Nickson
Cover Designer: Kim Wedlake

Library of Congress Cataloging–in–Publication Data

A collection of twentieth century American short stories Volume 2/[compiled by] Jean A. McConochie.
    p. cm.
  ISBN 0–8384–6146–8
  1. English language—Textbooks for foreign speakers. 2. United States—Social life and customs—20th century—Fiction. 3. Short stories, American. 4. Readers.   I. McConochie, Jean A.
PE1128.A56 1994
813' .010805—dc20   94–43027
                                                          CIP

Heinle & Heinle Publishers is a division of International Thomson Publishing, Inc.

Manufactured in the United States of America.

ISBN 0-8384-4851-8

10 9 8 7 6 5 4 3 2 1

For my mother,
Marian Brenckle McConochie,
who introduced me to the enchantment of literature

Contents

Introduction

Ernest Hemingway, **Hills Like White Elephants**   1
*"They just let the air in and then it's all perfectly
natural."*

Leslie Marmon Silko, **The Man to Send Rain Clouds** 15
*"About the priest sprinkling holy water for
Grandpa. So he won't be thirsty."*

Danny Santiago, **The Somebody**   31
*A spray can has no heart. The letters come out
very dead.*

Toshio Mori, **Japanese Hamlet**   49
*"Some day I'll be the ranking Shakespearean
actor," he said.*

Judy Troy, **Secrets**   63
*. . . my life had started to seem like too much
trouble.*

John Updike, **The Orphaned Swimming Pool**   79
*True, late splashes and excited guffaws did often
keep Mrs. Chace awake, ...*

Carson McCullers, **The Sojourner**   91
*Certainly his love for his ex-wife was long since
past. So why the unhinged body, the shaken mind?*

Contents

Lucy Honig, **English as a Second Language**   109
*"And Mama, you are going for an award in
English, for all you've learned, so please speak
English!"*

W.D. Wetherell, **The Bass, the River, and Shelia
Mant**   131
*There was a summer in my life when the only
creature lovelier to me than a largemouth bass
was Shelia Mant.*

Andrea Lee, **Fine Points**   147
*A few years earlier, it might have been possible for
me to find the necessary thrill simply in going out
with white boys, the forbidden fruit of my mother's
generation; . . . .*

Mark Steven Hess, **Where You Have Been, Where
You Are Going**   163
*"How long were you in jail?" I ask through everyone's
laughter. Grandfather keeps an even expression.*

Donald Hall, **Christmas Snow**   179
*First, standing in the doorway but still outside, he
stripped three gloves from each hand and tossed them
ahead of him into the shed.*

Introduction

Twentieth Century American Short Stories, Volume 1, is one of three related publications designed to introduce English-as-a-second or foreign language students to the richness and variety of modern American short fiction. The complete program includes:

- *Twentieth Century American Short Stories*, Volume 1   high intermediate

- *Twentieth Century American Short Sories*, Volume 2   advanced

- *Twentieth Century American Short Stories*, An Anthology   a collection of all of the stories from Volumes 1 and 2, without the activities

How THE STORIES HAVE BEEN CHOSEN

While the choices necessarily reflect the editor's tastes, the selections are intended to suggest the cultural and ethnic diversity of twentieth-century American fiction. Some of the stories in this book are humorous; others are serious. Some are set in large cities—New York, Chicago, Los Angeles; others take place in suburban or rural areas of New England, the South, the Midwest, or the West. Together, the stories explore universal questions of relations within families and between the sexes, changing customs and traditions, and conflicts of culture that aren't always recognized by those involved. All are superb tales that can be read again and again with increasing pleasure.

All of the stories are relatively short, ranging in length from approximately five hundred to approximately six thousand words. They are appropriate in content and vocabulary for high-intermediate (Volume 1) or advanced (Volume 2) students of English as a second or foreign language. The stories are also suitable for high school or college students whose first language is English, though they would probably find the "Uncommon Words or Meanings" section unnecessary.

The selections are from all but the first two decades of the twentieth century, with half of the stories in Volume 1 and three-quarters of those in Volume 2 published after mid-century. All of the twenty-four stories represent an American point of view, though two stories are set outside the United States, two are by British authors who place their stories in an American context, and five of the twenty-four authors spoke another language before they learned English. While many of the stories have been translated into other languages, all of them were originally written in English.

How This Edition Differs from the First Edition

Of the nine stories in the first edition, five have been kept for Volume 1: "The Unicorn in the Garden" by James Thurber, "The Chaser" by John Collier, "Love" by Jesse Stuart, "The Use of Force" by William Carlos Williams, and "The Lottery" by Shirley Jackson. "The Orphaned Swimming Pool" by John Updike appears in Volume 2, as does Ernest Hemingway's "Hills Like White Elephants," which has been substituted for his story "The Killers."

For each author, the biographical material has been expanded and now forms part of the introduction to the story. The glossary now precedes the story, with no interruption of the text to indicate glossed words, and with objective criteria for choosing words to be glossed. Grammar and vocabulary exercises have been replaced by questions concerned with style and with connections between and among stories.

How the Volumes Are Organized

The stories in Volume 1 are, on average, slightly shorter and simpler in structure and vocabulary than those in Volume 2. Within each volume, the stories have been ordered by increasing complexity of plot and vocabulary, with an eye to balance in content, tone, and style. However, while there is some cross-referencing in the "Making Connections" questions, the stories otherwise function as self-contained units.

The **Introduction** to each story presents the author in the context of his or her time and previews the story. Where appropriate, it also includes suggestions for further reading.

Unusual Words or Meanings provides brief explanations of words that can't easily be found in a dictionary: cultural references (such as brand and place names), idioms, slang, words in languages other than English, and words used in a meaning other than the most common (here defined as the first meaning listed in the *Oxford Advanced Learner's Dictionary*, Third Edition). Words are defined only as they are used in the story and are presented in the order in which they appear in the story. Nouns are glossed in their singular form, preceded by *a* or *an* if the noun is countable, and time-oriented verbs are glossed in their *to* (infinitive) form.

Each **story** is presented as the author wrote it: nothing has been simplified; any extra space between paragraphs was put there by the author; the presence or absence of quotation marks for direct speech is the author's choice. While words glossed in the "Unusual Words or Meanings" section are not marked in the text, line numbers have been added in the margin to facilitate discussion. Following the convention of many literature texts, the original publication date appears in square brackets at the end of the story.

Understanding the Story questions, rather than asking for simple facts, require synthesis and analysis. Their purpose is to direct readers back to the story, encouraging careful reading. This and the following sections also provide an opportunity for students to explore the uses of several literary terms that are commonly used by college-educated speakers of English, including *allusion, connotation, foreshadowing, irony, metaphor, personification, simile,* and *stereotype*. The literary terms are briefly defined the first time they are used in a chapter with the aim of helping readers to become comfortable with the terms and how they are used.

Developing a Way with Words offers a closer look at a stylistic aspect of the story, examining sentences that share a common element or exploring questions of vocabulary usage.

Making Connections provides a wide range of options for discussion, with most of the topics also being suitable as points of departure for writing. Readers may be invited to speculate on the characters, to dramatize the story, to explore a related story or poem, to write a letter, to analyze some aspect of plot or imagery, to compare and contrast the story with one previously read in class, or to connect the story with events in their own lives. The topics are at varying levels of complexity, so that teachers and students in a particular class may choose the one or two topics best suited to their needs. If there is a film or video version of the story, information on it forms the basis for the last question of this section.

If readers want to read more when they have finished these stories, the books' purpose will have been achieved.

Acknowledgements

Many friends and colleagues have helped to make this book a reality. Indeed, the collaborative aspect was the greatest pleasure in preparing the manuscript. It is now my honor to name those who have contributed their talents and supportive concern to the project.

David R. Werner provided superb coaching at every stage of writing and production; his intelligence, understanding, and sense of humor have enriched the book. All in all, Dave and the boys kept both me and Mike (my computer) running smoothly throughout the process. My thanks for it all.

Winifred A. Falcon, Karla Jay, Laurie Lafferty, Jaime Mantilla, and Brett Sherman, as well as Heinle & Heinle readers, all helped in shaping the final selection of stories. Anne McCormick offered invaluable support in pursuing permissions, which are gratefully acknowledged at the back of the book. In addition, the authors Mari Evans, Mark Steven Hess, Lucy Honig, Judy Troy, W. D. Wetherell, and Hisaye Yamamoto responded graciously and generously to the queries of a stranger. My thanks to them, and indeed to all the writers whose stories and poems have provided me with such intense pleasure over the past two years.

Laurie Lafferty and Dave Werner patiently read successive drafts; their creative criticism and perceptive comments strengthened every chapter. One or more chapters also benefitted from the insights of Winnie Falcon, Jaime Mantilla, and Pat Rigg, as well as my editor Amy Lawler, and the following reviewers commissioned by Heinle & Heinle:

Lynne Barsky, *Suffolk Community College, New York*
Meggie Courtright, *University of Illinois, Urbana-Champaign*
Kay Ferrell, *Rancho Santiago Community College, California*
Judith Garcia, *Miami-Dade Community College*
Thomas Hardy, *University of Southern Mississippi*
Virginia Herringer, *Pasadena City College*
Joe McVeigh, *University of Southern California*
Melissa Munroe, *Boston University*
Karen Richelli-Kolbert, *Manhattanville College*
Ross Savage, *North Hennepin Community College,
    Minnesota*
Diane Starke, *El Paso Community College*
Mark Stepner, *Boston University*
Mo-Shuet Tam, *San Francisco Community College*

Additional field-testing was generously provided by Lise
Winer and her Southern Illinois University graduate students Lori
Brown, Tenley Chambliss, Randy Cotten, Simone DeVito, Laura
Halliday, Robert Lee, and Paula Tabor, who tried many of the sto-
ries out with their undergraduate students. My thanks to all.

For additional clarification of assorted points, I am indebted
to Judith Bauduy, Paul Cochran, Sergio Gaitán, Janet Ghattas,
John Lafferty, George Marino, Shirley Miller, Tina Pratt, Allan
Rabinowitz, Muriel Shine, Tippy Schwabe, and Patricia and Sid-
ney Wittenberg, as well as to Jane Knowles, reference librarian at
Radcliffe College. At Pace University's Henry Birnbaum Library, I
benefitted from the creative determination of reference librari-
ans Michelle Fanelli, and Tom Snyder and from the legacy of the
late Bruce Bergman, whose passion for acquisition has enriched
us all.

Also at Pace University, Sherman Raskin, chair, Department
of English, offered unstinting encouragement throughout the
manuscript preparation, and Charles Masiello, dean, Dyson College of Arts and Sciences, kindly granted me a one-semester sab-
batical leave to complete the manuscript. My thanks to both of
them.

At Heinle & Heinle, Erik Gundersen proposed this revision
and expansion of the original text, Amy Lawler tactfully suggested editorial improvements, Kristin Thalheimer and Margaret
Cleveland meticulously supervised production, and Andreas Mar-
tin developed a creative marketing plan. I am grateful to all of

them for enabling me to benefit from their professional expertise. For friendly and reliable technical support, Sanford Fox and his crew at Foxy Copy were, as always, indispensible.

The initial impetus for this book came, many years ago, from my colleague and friend Gary Gabriel, whom I thank once again.

Hills Like White Elephants

"'They just let the

air in and then it's

all perfectly

natural.'"

Hills Like
White Elephants

Ernest Hemingway
(1899–1961)

Ernest Hemingway almost single-handedly set the tone for twentieth-century American fiction. On the surface, his much-imitated style seems very easy to read and write. However, Hemingway challenges his readers to sense the emotion behind the words and to listen for the thoughts that the words either conceal or unintentionally (on the speaker's part) reveal.

Hemingway grew up in comfortable circumstances in Oak Park, Illinois, a suburb of Chicago. The family spent summers at their vacation home in Michigan, where young Ernest learned to hunt and fish. These activities reflected his ambitious and competitive spirit and remained important to him throughout his life. He found his way into World War I by convincing his father to let him volunteer as an ambulance driver for the American Red Cross in Italy. Six weeks after arriving in Italy, and two weeks before his nineteenth birthday, Hemingway was wounded under fire, thereby becoming something of a hero. He had long thrived on the companionship and admiration of other men; recovering from his wounds at the American Red Cross Hospital in Milan, he learned how attractive he was to women as well.

Hemingway returned to the U.S. briefly, married the first of his four wives, then returned to Europe. Living in Paris, he worked as a correspondent for the Toronto *Star* and established his position as one of the most celebrated writers of his generation. The novels he wrote during this time are modern classics, two of the most famous being *The Sun*

Also Rises (1926), about British and American expatriates in Paris and Spain, and *A Farewell to Arms* (1929), about doomed lovers in Italy during World War I. The heroes of these novels show physical courage in the face of danger, exemplifying Hemingway's admiration for "grace under pressure." The conversational style of his characters seems surprisingly modern. It can be said that Hemingway's characters, with their terse speech and lack of overt emotional involvement, served to define what is "cool" and American. Marlon Brando and James Dean would later personify this style in movies, and in turn would be imitated by teenagers to this day. The works also explore the complex relations between men and women, which seemed to puzzle Hemingway through all of his four marriages.

Fiction must be based on actual experience, Hemingway insisted, for "a writer's job is to tell the truth" and a good story "should produce a truer account than anything factual can be." According to the report of one of his friends,* Hemingway got the idea for "Hills Like White Elephants" (from Hemingway's 1927 collection *Men Without Women*) during an evening with American colleagues in an Italian café. They were speaking of birth control and of the cruelty of laws that made it a crime for a young unmarried woman to end an unwanted pregnancy. The man in the party who later wrote about it remembered an experience from his college days. At a time when abortion was both illegal and a forbidden topic in polite company, a young woman had spoken casually of having had an abortion. "Oh, it was nothing," the man remembered her saying. "The doctor just let the air in and a few hours later it was over." Four years later, Hemingway told the man that his remark had suggested the story "Hills Like White Elephants."

In what way could an American writer approach a subject that was shocking to many Americans at the time? And if the subject couldn't be discussed openly, how could the sentences in the story be—as Hemingway insisted they must be—"true"?

---

* Robert McAlmon, *Being Geniuses Together;* quoted by Carlos Baker in the major Hemingway biography to date—*Ernest Hemingway: A Life Story,* 1969.

Uncommon Words or Meanings

Words or phrases from the story are explained if they are cultural references (including words in a language other than English), idioms, or slang, or if the meaning is not the first listed in a standard dictionary. The words or phrases appear in their order of first use in the story.

Ebro ("the valley of the *Ebro*")—a river in north-central Spain, about 150 miles north of Madrid.

a girl ("the American and the *girl* with him")—at the time this story was written, "girl" was commonly used to refer to any female who was not distinctly elderly.

a white elephant ("Hills Like *White Elephants*")—an expression used to describe something that is useless and expensive to keep but seems too valuable to throw away.

a real ("Four *reales.*")—a Spanish coin.

Anis del Toro ("We want two *Anis del Toro.*")—a brand of Spanish liqueur flavored with anise seed, which has a slightly bitter, slightly sweet taste. Anise seed is also the flavoring in **licorice,** a chewy black candy.

absinthe ("all the things you've waited so long for, like *absinthe*")—a French liqueur also flavored with anise seed. Since 1915, it has been illegal to produce absinthe in France because another ingredient, wormwood, has been found to cause delirium, hallucinations, and ultimately death.

bright ("I said the mountains looked like white elephants. Wasn't that *bright*?")—clever, original.

to cut (something) out ("Oh, *cut it out.*")—(idiom) to stop doing or saying (something that is annoying).

awfully ("an *awfully* simple operation")—very.

to let . . . in—("It's just to *let* the air *in.*")—to allow something to enter.

Hills Like White Elephants

The hills across the valley of the Ebro were long and white. On this side there was no shade and no trees and the station was between two lines of rails in the sun. Close against the side of the station there was the warm shadow of the building and a curtain, made of strings of bamboo beads, hung across the open door into the bar, to keep out flies. The American and the girl with him sat at a table in the shade, outside the building. It was very hot and the express from Barcelona would come in forty minutes. It stopped at this junction for two minutes and went on to Madrid.

"What should we drink?" the girl asked. She had taken off her hat and put it on the table.

"It's pretty hot," the man said.

"Let's drink beer."

"Dos cervzas," the man said into the curtain.

"Big ones?" a woman asked from the doorway.

"Yes. Two big ones."

The woman brought two glasses of beer and two felt pads. She put the felt pads and the beer glasses on the table and looked at the man and the girl. The girl was looking off at the line of hills. They were white in the sun and the country was brown and dry.

"They look like white elephants," she said.

"I've never seen one," the man drank his beer.

"No, you wouldn't have."

"I might have," the man said. "Just because you say I wouldn't have doesn't prove anything."

The girl looked at the bead curtain. "They've painted something on it," she said. "What does it say?"

"Anis del Toro. It's a drink."

"Could we try it?"

The man called "Listen" through the curtain. The woman came out from the bar.

"Four reales."

"We want two Anis del Tor."

"With water?"

"Do you want it with water?"

"I don't know," the girl said. "Is it good with water?"

"It's all right."

"You want them with water?" asked the woman.

"Yes, with water."

"It tastes like licorice," the girl said and put the glass down.

"That's the way with everything."

"Yes," said the girl. "Everything tastes of licorice. Especially all the things you've waited so long for, like absinthe."

"Oh, cut it out."

"You started it," the girl said. "I was being amused. I was having a fine time."

"Well, let's try and have a fine time."

"All right. I was trying. I said the mountains looked like white elephants. Wasn't that bright?"

"That was bright."

"I wanted to try this new drink. That's all we do, isn't it—look at things and try new drinks?"

"I guess so."

The girl looked across at the hills.

"They're lovely hills," she said. "They don't really look like white elephants. I just meant the coloring of their skin through the trees."

"Should we have another drink?"

"All right."

The warm wind blew the bead curtain against the table.

"The beer's nice and cool," the man said.

"It's lovely," the girl said.

"It's really an awfully simple operation, Jig," the man said. "It's not really an operation at all."

The girl looked at the ground the table legs rested on.

"I know you wouldn't mind it, Jig. It's really not anything. It's just to let the air in."

The girl did not say anything.

"I'll go with you and I'll stay with you all the time. They just let the air in and then it's all perfectly natural."

"Then what will we do afterward?"

"We'll be fine afterward. Just like we were before."

"What makes you think so?"

"That's the only thing that bothers us. It's the only thing that's made us unhappy."

The girl looked at the bead curtain, put her hand out and took hold of two of the strings of beads.

80   "And you think then we'll be all right and be happy."

"I know we will. You don't have to be afraid. I've known lots of people that have done it."

"So have I," said the girl. "And afterward they were all so happy."

85   "Well," the man said, "if you don't want to you don't have to. I wouldn't have you do it if you didn't want to. But I know it's perfectly simple."

"And you really want to?"

"I think it's the best thing to do. But I don't want you to do

90 it if you don't really want to."

"And if I do it you'll be happy and things will be like they were and you'll love me?"

"I love you now. You know I love you."

"I know. But if I do it, then it will be nice again if I say

95 things are like white elephants, and you'll like it?"

"I'll love it. I love it now but I just can't think about it. You know how I get when I worry."

"If I do it you won't ever worry?"

"I won't worry about that because it's perfectly simple."

100   "Then I'll do it. Because I don't care about me."

"What do you mean?"

"I don't care about me."

"Well, I care about you."

"Oh yes. But I don't care about me. And I'll do it and then

105 everything will be fine."

"I don't want you to do it if you feel that way."

The girl stood up and walked to the end of the station. Across, on the other side, were fields of grain and trees along the banks of the Ebro. Far away, beyond the river, were moun-

110 tains. The shadow of a cloud moved across the field of grain and she saw the river through the trees.

"And we could have all this," she said. "And we could have everything and every day we make it more impossible."

"What did you say?"

115   "I said we could have everything."

"We can have everything."

"No, we can't."

"We can have the whole world."

"No, we can't."

120   "We can go everywhere."

"No, we can't. It isn't ours any more."

"It's ours."

"No, it isn't. And once they take it away, you never get it back."

125   "But they haven't taken it away."

"We'll wait and see."

"Come on back in the shade," he said. "You mustn't feel that way."

"I don't feel any way," the girl said. "I just know things."

130   "I don't want you to do anything that you don't want to do—"

"Nor that isn't good for me," she said. "I know. Could we have another beer?"

"All right. But you've got to realize—"

135   "I realize," the girl said. "Can't we maybe stop talking?"

They sat down at the table and the girl looked across at the hills on the dry side of the valley and the man looked at her and at the table.

"You've got to realize," he said, "that I don't want you to do

140   it if you don't want to. I'm perfectly willing to go through with it if it means anything to you."

"Doesn't it mean anything to you? We could get along."

"Of course it does. But I don't want anybody but you. I don't want any one else. And I know it's perfectly simple."

145   "Yes, you know it's perfectly simple."

"It's all right for you to say that, but I do know it."

"Would you do something for me now?"

"I'd do anything for you."

"Would you please please please please please please please stop talking?"

150   He did not say anything but looked at the bags against the wall of the station. There were labels on them from all the hotels where they had spent nights.

"But I don't want you to," he said, "I don't care anything

155   about it."

"I'll scream," the girl said.

The woman came out through the curtains with two glasses of beer and put them down on the damp felt pads. "The train comes in five minutes," she said.

Ernest Hemingway

160   "What did she say?" asked the girl.

"That the train is coming in five minutes."

The girl smiled brightly at the woman, to thank her.

"I'd better take the bags over to the other side of the station," the man said. She smiled at him.

165   "All right. Then come back and we'll finish the beer."

He picked up the two heavy bags and carried them around the station to the other tracks. He looked up the tracks but could not see the train. Coming back, he walked through the barroom, where people waiting for the train were drinking. He

170 drank an Anis at the bar and looked at the people. They were all waiting reasonably for the train. He went out through the bead curtain. She was sitting at the table and smiled at him.

"Do you feel better?" he asked.

"I feel fine," she said. "There's nothing wrong with me. I

175 feel fine."

[1925]

Understanding the Story

These questions call for analysis and synthesis of the story's main points.

1. Early in the story, the young woman says (lines 53–54), "That's all we do—look at things and try new drinks." Close to the end of the story, the young man looks at their suitcases, which had "labels from all the hotels where they had spent nights" (lines 152–53). What do the quoted words tell the reader about the nature of the couple's travels? In Spain, how might it make a difference to them that the young man speaks Spanish but Jig doesn't?

2. In the following exchange (lines 23–27), what tone do you think each person uses? Is it a friendly or unfriendly exchange?

"They look like white elephants," she said.

"I've never seen one," the man drank his beer.

"No, you wouldn't have."

"I might have," the man said. "Just because you say I wouldn't have doesn't prove anything."

3. "Everything tastes of licorice," the young woman says. "Especially all the things you've waited so long for, like absinthe" (lines 44–45).

    a. How does licorice taste?

    b. What "things" beside tasting absinthe might she have been waiting to experience?

4. What is the "operation" that they keep referring to?

    a. Why are they speaking about it so indirectly?

    b. What is the basis for the man's certainly that the operation is "perfectly simple"?

    c. Why does he think that she is hesitant to have it? Is he right? How do you know?

5. The action of the story turns (line 134) when the young man starts to say that Jig must realize something and she interrupts him. (He takes up his remark again in line 139.)

    a. How did the young man intend to finish his sentence?

    b. What has Jig realized?

6. What tone do you think each person uses in the exchange that begins with the young man resuming his thought and ends with Jig's dramatic string of "pleases" (lines 149–50)?

7. Whose point of view is reflected in the comment (lines 170–71), "They were all waiting reasonably for the train"? From the same point of view, who, by implication, was acting unreasonably?

8. What answer does the young man expect to his final question (line 173)? What does Jig suggest by her three-sentence response?

9. The title is a simile (a direct comparison) implying that a range of hills looks like a herd of white elephants.

a. What is the literal reference of the title? That is, where in the story are specific hills compared to white elephants?

b. What is the metaphorical sense (the implied or suggested comparison) of hills and white elephants? What besides the hills is white and rounded? What "white elephant"—a valuable but unwanted possession—do the young man and woman have?

Developing a Way with Words

For those who wish to look more closely at how a story has been told, this section presents either distinctive features of the author's style, or, for a few stories, a related literary text.

1. In the following conversations, identify the meaning of "it" each time the word is used. At what points does the young man shift the meaning of "it"? At what points does Jig shift the meaning of "it?" At each of these points, are they both aware of the shift?

a. "The beer's nice and cool," the man said.

"**It**'s lovely," the girl said.

"**It**'s really an awfully simple operation, Jig," the man said. "**It**'s not really an operation at all." (lines 63–66)

b. "We can have the whole world."

"No, we can't."

"We can go everywhere."

"No, we can't. **It** isn't ours any more."

"**It**'s ours."

"No, **it** isn't. And once they take **it** away, you never get **it** back."

"But they haven't taken **it** away."

"We'll wait and see." (lines 118–26)

c. "You've got to realize," he said, "that I don't want you to do **it** if you don't want to. I'm perfectly willing to go through with **it** if **it** means anything to you."

"Doesn't **it** mean anything to you? . . ."

"Of course **it** does. . . . And I know **it's** perfectly simple." (lines 139–44)

2. Consider the role of the setting in this story.

a. How is the scenery different on the two sides of the station (see lines 1–2 and 108–11)? How does that difference reflect the young couple's situation?

b. The cafe is at a railroad junction, a place where two railway lines meet and cross. What metaphorical (figurative, not literal) junction has the couple come to?

3. Hemingway is noted for the "economy" of his prose, for how much he is able to leave out and still tell a story. For example, he commonly leaves out such phrases as "he said casually" or "Jig said in a worried tone."

a. As a class, take the exchanges in lines 71–77 and add phrases like "he said casually" to identify the speaker and emotion for each line. Then discuss how the additions affect the tone of the story.

b. Working in small groups, add similar phrases for the exchanges in lines 88–97 or lines 98–106. Then compare and discuss your choices.

Making Connections

The options for discussion and writing (at varying levels of complexity) invite readers to connect the stories with their own experience and with other works of literature.

1. This story takes place in the 1920s.

a. Does it surprise you that an unmarried couple, both young Americans, were traveling together in Spain at that time? Can you imagine the story being set in another country or with a couple of a different nationality?

b. It was uncommon for unmarried couples to travel together at that time. How common is it now?

c. What reasons might there be for a man and woman who are not married to travel together?

2. At the beginning of the story, the young man insists that he loves Jig, while she says that she doesn't care about herself. If a female friend of yours told you the same thing about her relationship with her boyfriend and asked for your comments, what would you say to her?

3. Do you agree with the young man that their relationship will be "fine" (line 74) if Jig agrees to the operation? Why or why not?

4. Read the story as a play. Dividing the story into three scenes requires eleven actors (with speaking parts) and three directors (to keep track of who should be speaking and to help the actors decide how to say their lines). This can be done as a whole class, with the teacher taking the three director roles or in three small groups. In the latter case, each group could be responsible for presenting one scene to the whole class.

Scene 1, from the beginning through line 55 ("I guess so"). Five roles: NARRATOR (1 short and 2 long descriptive passages), MAN (15 speeches), JIG (12 speeches), WOMAN (3 speeches), and DIRECTOR.

Scene 2, from line 56 (The girl looked across the hills.) through line 106 ("I don't want you to do it if you feel that way."). Four roles: NARRATOR (3 short descriptive passages), MAN (15 speeches), JIG (14 speeches), and DIRECTOR.

Scene 3, from line 107 (The girl stood up and walked to the end of the station.) to the end of the story. Five roles: NARRATOR (5 descriptive passages), MAN (17 speeches), WOMAN (1 speech—in Spanish), JIG (18 speeches), and DIRECTOR.

5. The characters in this story avoid speaking directly about an important issue. When you want to talk to someone close to you (for example, your mother, father, husband, or wife), do you choose a special time and place? How do you bring up the idea—directly or indirectly? As an option for writing, think about a time when you had to discuss an important issue with someone close to you; describe the experience.

The Man to Send Rain Clouds

"'About the priest

sprinkling holy

water for Grandpa.

So he won't be

thirsty.'"

The Man to Send Rain Clouds

Leslie Marmon Silko
(born 1948)

Leslie Marmon Silko, who now lives in Tucson, Arizona, grew up in New Mexico in the Laguna Pueblo, the largest of the Rio Grande Pueblo Indian communities. (Laguna had a population of close to three thousand in the 1960s.) Like many Southwesterners, Silko's ancestry includes white speakers of English, Mexican speakers of Spanish, and American Indians. As a child, Silko loved listening to the stories told by her Laguna grandmother and great-aunt. "The best thing you can have in life," she has told an interviewer, "is to have someone tell you a story."* Years later, in her first creative writing class in college, Silko found she had so many ideas that she hardly knew where to begin. "The Man to Send Rain Clouds," which was based on an actual event at Laguna, was written during her college years. Silko's work gained national attention when that story, along with others of hers, appeared in 1974 in *The Man to Send Rain Clouds,* edited by Kenneth Rosen, one of the first anthologies of fiction written by American Indians. A collection of Silko's stories and poems was published as *Storyteller* (1981). In addition, she has published the novels *Ceremony* (1977) and *Almanac of the Dead* (1991), the latter written with the support of a MacArthur Foundation "genius" grant. All of Silko's fiction is concerned with the struggle of American Indians to live in two worlds, maintaining their traditional culture within the context of modern life.

*In Laura Coltelli, *Winged Words: American Indian Writers Speak* (1990).

The first American Indians arrived between 29,000 and 22,000 years ago, in a series of Ice Age of migrations from Asia. By 2000 B.C., some of those prehistoric immigrants were living in what is now the American Southwest. Fourteen centuries later, their descendants had settled in permanent villages with multi-story dwellings. When Spanish explorers arrived in the mid-1500s, they used *pueblo,* the Spanish word for "village" or "town," as their name for all the American Indian peoples of the region; that usage was later borrowed by English-speakers.

The Spanish brought with them diseases and a hunger for gold, with sad results that are well known. They also brought the Franciscan order of missionary priests, who were charged by the Pope to "save souls in the New World." The Franciscans, with the best and worst of intentions, gradually imposed the beliefs and rituals of Roman Catholicism on the "pagan" American Indians. In public, the Pueblos practiced the new European religion; in private they continued to follow their own religion, making sure that the ceremonies and beliefs were never revealed to outsiders. Understandably, one result was mutual wariness and a great potential for misunderstanding. In "The Man to Send Rain Clouds," this situation is presented in the context of differing beliefs about death and funeral customs. Who beyond family members needs to be told right away when someone has died? What ceremonies must be followed in disposing of a dead body? And what could a death have to do with life-giving rain?

Uncommon Words or Meanings

a cottonwood tree ("under a big *cottonwood* tree")—the poplar, a tree with cottonlike tufts of white hair on its tiny seeds; the Southwestern varieties of the tree grow alongside streams.

an arroyo ("grew in the wide, sandy *arroyo*")—in the Southwestern United States, the dry bed of a stream.

to squint ("he *squinted* up at the sun")—to look with the eyes partly closed.

corn meal, corn pollen ("throw pinches of *corn meal and pollen*")—two forms of corn, both of which have religious significance for the Pueblos and would be carried in a medicine bag. "Corn meal" is coarsely ground dried corn; "corn pollen" is the fine yellowish powder on the silky strands of an ear of corn.

a tarp ("covered it with a heavy *tarp*")—short for "tarpaulin," a sheet of canvas or other strong waterproof material, used as a protective covering.

Father ("saw *Father* Paul's car")—"Father" is the term of address for a Roman Catholic priest.

the Angelus ("the church bells rang the *Angelus*")—a prayer said by Roman Catholics at morning, noon, and night.

clanspeople ("the neighbors and *clanspeople*")—members of the same clan, a group of relatives. The clans conduct religious ceremonies.

a medicine bag ("their candles and *medicine bags*")—a small leather or fabric sack used to carry small religious objects and corn pollen.

a pickup ("the body was laid into the *pickup*")—short for "pickup truck," a small light truck with an open back.

holy water ("sprinkling *holy water*")—water blessed by a priest for religious uses.

the Lamb ("its symbols of the *Lamb*")—with a capital letter, a Christian symbol for Jesus, "the Lamb of God," in the sense of a baby sheep who is sacrificed as an offering to God on behalf of a community.

cloister ("the nuns' *cloister* across the patio")—a building where nuns live in religious seclusion.

the Last Rites ("I could have brought the *Last Rites*")—the popular name for a ceremony performed by a Roman Catholic priest when a person is dying.

a tumbleweed ("the yellow, dry, *tumbleweeds*")—in the desert of the southwestern U.S., a plant that breaks off from its roots and is then blown about by the wind.

squash flowers ("the wilted *squash flowers*")—the large flower of a vinelike plant of the gourd family, one of the basic foods of the Pueblo culture; the flower grows limp from lack of water.

Franciscan ("the priest's brown *Franciscan* robe")—a religious order, for both men and women, founded by St. Francis of Assisi and dedicated to serving the poor and the sick. The Franciscans were the dominant order of missionaries in North America.

a pueblo ("off the highway onto the sandy *pueblo* road")—in the Southwestern United States, particularly the Rio Grande valley, an American Indian village.

The Man to Send Rain Clouds

ONE

They found him under a big cottonwood tree. His Levi jacket and pants were faded light-blue so that he had been easy to find. The big cottonwood tree stood apart from a small
5 grove of winterbare cottonwoods which grew in the wide, sandy arroyo. He had been dead for a day or more, and the sheep had wandered and scattered up and down the arroyo. Leon and his brother-in-law, Ken, gathered the sheep and left them in the pen at the sheep camp before they returned to the
10 cottonwood tree. Leon waited under the tree while Ken drove the truck through the deep sand to the edge of the arroyo. He squinted up at the sun and unzipped his jacket—it sure was hot for this time of year. But high and northwest the blue mountains were still deep in snow. Ken came sliding down the
15 low, crumbling bank about fifty yards down, and he was bringing the red blanket.

Before they wrapped the old man, Leon took a piece of string out of his pocket and tied a small gray feather in the old man's long white hair. Ken gave him the paint. Across the
20 brown wrinkled forehead he drew a streak of white and along the high cheekbones he drew a strip of blue paint. He paused and watched Ken throw pinches of corn meal and pollen into the wind that fluttered the small gray feather. Then Leon painted with yellow under the old man's broad nose, and
25 finally, when he had painted green across the chin, he smiled.

"Send us rain clouds, Grandfather." They laid the bundle in the back of the pickup and covered it with a heavy tarp before they started back to the pueblo.

They turned off the highway onto the sandy pueblo road.
30 Not long after they passed the store and post office they saw Father Paul's car coming toward them. When he recognized their faces he slowed his car and waved for them to stop. The young priest rolled down the car window.

"Did you find old Teofilo?" he asked loudly.
35 Leon stopped the truck. "Good morning, Father. We were just out to the sheep camp. Everything is O.K. now."

"Thank God for that. Teofilo is a very old man. You really shouldn't allow him to stay at the sheep camp alone."

"No, he won't do that any more now."

40   "Well, I'm glad you understand. I hope I'll be seeing you at Mass this week—we missed you last Sunday. See if you can get old Teofilo to come with you." The priest smiled and waved at them as they drove away.

TWO

45   Louise and Teresa were waiting. The table was set for lunch, and the coffee was boiling on the black iron stove. Leon looked at Louise and then at Teresa.

    "We found him under a cottonwood tree in the big arroyo near the sheep camp. I guess he sat down to rest in the shade
50 and never got up again." Leon walked toward the old man's bed. The red plaid shawl had been shaken and spread carefully over the bed, and a new brown flannel shirt and pair of stiff new Levis were arranged neatly beside the pillow. Louise held the screen door open while Leon and Ken carried in the red
55 blanket. He looked small and shriveled, and after they dressed him in the new shirt and pants he seemed more shrunken.

    It was noontime now because the church bells rang the Angelus. They ate the beans with hot bread, and nobody said anything until after Teresa poured the coffee.

60   Ken stood up and put on his jacket. "I'll see about the gravediggers. Only the top layer of soil is frozen. I think it can be ready before dark."

    Leon nodded his head and finished his coffee. After Ken had been gone for a while, the neighbors and clanspeople
65 came quietly to embrace Teofilo's family and to leave food on the table because the gravediggers would come to eat when they were finished.

THREE

    The sky in the west was full of pale-yellow light. Louise
70 stood outside with her hands in the pockets of Leon's green army jacket that was too big for her. The funeral was over, and the old men had taken their candles and medicine bags and were gone. She waited until the body was laid into the pickup before she said anything to Leon. She touched his arm, and he
75 noticed that her hands were still dusty from the corn meal that she had sprinkled around the old man. When she spoke, Leon could not hear her.

"What did you say? I didn't hear you."

"I said that I had been thinking about something."

"About what?"

"About the priest sprinkling holy water for Grandpa. So he won't be thirsty."

Leon stared at the new moccasins that Teofilo had made for the ceremonial dances in the summer. They were nearly hidden by the red blanket. It was getting colder, and the wind pushed gray dust down the narrow pueblo road. The sun was approaching the long mesa where it disappeared during the winter. Louise stood there shivering and watching his face. The he zipped up his jacket and opened the truck door. "I'll see if he's there."

FOUR

Ken stopped the pickup at the church, and Leon got out; and then Ken drove down the hill to the graveyard where people were waiting. Leon knocked at the old carved door with its symbols of the Lamb. While he waited he looked up at the twin bells from the king of Spain with the last sunlight pouring around them in their tower.

The priest opened the door and smiled when he saw who it was. "Come in! What brings you here this evening?"

The priest walked toward the kitchen, and Leon stood with his cap in his hand, playing with the earflaps and examining the living room—the brown sofa, the green armchair, and the brass lamp that hung down from the ceiling by links of chain. The priest dragged a chair out of the kitchen and offered it to Leon.

"No thank you, Father. I only came to ask you if you would bring your holy water to the graveyard."

The priest turned away from Leon and looked out the window at the patio full of shadows and the dining-room windows of the nuns' cloister across the patio. The curtains were heavy, and the light from within faintly penetrated; it was impossible to see the nuns inside eating supper. "Why didn't you tell me he was dead? I could have brought the Last Rites anyway."

Leon smiled. "It wasn't necessary, Father."

The priest stared down at his scuffed brown loafers and the worn hem of his cassock. "For a Christian burial it was necessary."

His voice was distant, and Leon thought that his blue eyes
120   looked tired.

"It's O.K. Father, we just want him to have plenty of water."

The priest sank down into the green chair and picked up a glossy missionary magazine. He turned the colored pages full
125   of lepers and pagans without looking at them.

"You know I can't do that, Leon. There should have been the Last Rites and funeral Mass at the very least."

Leon put on his green cap and pulled the flaps down over his ears. "It's getting late, Father. I've got to go."

130   When Leon opened the door Father Paul stood up and said, "Wait." He left the room and came back wearing a long brown overcoat. He followed Leon out the door and across the dim churchyard to the adobe steps in front of the church. They both stooped to fit through the low adobe entrance. And when
135   they started down the hill to the graveyard only half of the sun was visible above the mesa.

The priest approached the grave slowly, wondering how they had managed to dig into the frozen ground; and then he remembered that this was New Mexico, and saw the pile of
140   cold loose sand beside the hole. The people stood close to each other with little clouds of steam puffing from their faces. The priest looked at them and saw a pile of jackets, gloves, and scarves in the yellow, dry tumbleweeds that grew in the grave-yard. He looked at the red blanket, not sure that Teofilo was so
145   small, wondering if it wasn't some perverse Indian trick—something they did in March to ensure a good harvest—won-dering if maybe old Teofilo was actually at sheep camp corralling the sheep for the night. But there he was, facing into a cold dry wind and squinting at the last sunlight, ready to bury
150   a red wool blanket while the faces of his parishioners were in shadow with the last warmth of the sun on their backs.

His fingers were stiff, and it took him a long time to twist the lid off the holy water. Drops of water fell on the red blan-ket and soaked into dark icy spots. He sprinkled the grave and
155   the water disappeared almost before it touched the dim, cold sand; it reminded him of something—he tried to remember what it was, because he thought if he could remember he might understand this. He sprinkled more water; he shook the container until it was empty, and the water fell through the

160 light from the sundown like August rain that fell while the sun
was still shining, almost evaporating before it touched the
wilted squash flowers.

The wind pulled at the priest's brown Franciscan robe
and swirled away the corn meal and pollen that had been
165 sprinkled on the blanket. They lowered the bundle into the
ground, and they didn't bother to untie the stiff pieces of new
rope that were tied around the ends of the blanket. The sun
was gone, and over on the highway the eastbound lane was full
of headlights. The priest walked away slowly. Leon watched
170 him climb the hill, and when he had disappeared within the
tall, thick walls, Leon turned to look up at the high blue mountains in the deep snow that reflected a faint red light from the
west. He felt good because it was finished, and he was happy
about the sprinkling of the holy water; now the old man could
175 send them big thunderclouds for sure.

[1969]

Understanding the Story

1. The story opens with the sentence "They found him
   under a big cottonwood tree." Who is "he"? Who are
   "they"? What was "he" doing under the tree?

2. What evidence in the first two paragraphs shows that
   Leon and Ken were prepared for Teofilo's death? What
   ritual did they follow in caring for the body? Why do you
   think there is no explanation of what the ritual means?

3. What is the humorous irony (a difference between what
   is intended and what is understood) in the exchange
   (lines 34–43) when Leon and Ken meet Father Paul?
   Why do you think Leon didn't tell the young priest that
   Teofilo was dead?

4. In section TWO, what shows that Teofilo's family had
   anticipated his death? What funeral customs are mentioned there and in the first paragraph of section
   THREE? Why do you suppose Louise "sprinkled" corn
   meal, a sacred substance for the Pueblos, "around the
   old man" (line 76)? Why does she want the priest to

sprinkle holy water, a Roman Catholic symbol of blessing, when Teofilo is buried?

5. Leon's visit to Father Paul shows us more about the priest.

   a. Father Paul "dragged a chair out of the kitchen and offered it to Leon" (lines 104–05) when inviting him to sit down in the living room? Why do you suppose the priest didn't invite Leon to sit on the sofa or armchair in the room?

   b. What do you think was going through Father Paul's mind as he looked across at the nuns' cloister (lines 108–12)?

   c. What is suggested by the details of his "scuffed brown loafers" (line 116), and his "distant" voice and "tired" blue eyes (lines 119–20)?

6. What reason did Father Paul give for refusing Leon's request for holy water? Why do you think Leon didn't ask him to change his mind? And why did Father Paul change his mind on his own?

7. What does Father Paul's reaction to the burial (lines 137–51) tell us about his relation to the community?

   a. . . . then he remembered that this was New Mexico, . . .

      Why did Father Paul have to "remember" where he was?

   b. . . . wondering if it wasn't some perverse Indian trick . . .

      What is the connotation (the emotional suggestion) of "perverse"?

      What "trick" did Father Paul think the Indians might be playing on him?

   c. . . . something they did in March to ensure a good harvest . . .

      In a pagan culture, how might a funeral be related to a good harvest?

d. . . . ready to bury a red wool blanket . . .

   Does it matter to Father Paul, at this point, if Teofilo is really wrapped in the blanket? Does Father Paul see the blanket's ceremonial significance? For both questions, how do you know?

8. When Father Paul sprinkled the holy water, "it reminded him of something" (line 156) that he tried to remember "because he thought if he could remember he might understand this" (lines 157–58). What do you suppose the "something" was? What is the "this" that he was trying to understand?

9. Who would have sprinkled "the corn meal and pollen" (line 164) on the blanket? Why was it important to Teofilo's family to have both the water and the corn sprinkled on the grave?

10. From Father Paul's earlier thoughts and the description of him "walk[ing] away slowly" (line 169), how do you think he felt at the end of the ceremony? How did Leon feel? What would account for the difference in the men's reactions to the ceremony?

Developing a Way with Words

1. Using the (the "definite article") with a noun indicates that the noun refers to something known to both the speaker and listener. (For example, in the statement "Silko wrote the story," the speaker assumes that the listener knows which story is being referred to.) Yet, with no previous reference to blankets or paint, we are told that Ken "was bringing **the** red blanket" (lines 15–16) and that Ken gave Leon "**the** paint" (line 19). At the end of the story, there is a reference to the importance of August rain in reviving "**the** wilted squash flowers" (lines 161–62).

a. What does the narrator assume that the audience knows?

b. How does that technique make us, as readers, feel like members of the tribe? That is, how does it encourage us to share the viewpoint of Leon and Ken?

2. In the story, there are many contrasts between the Indians and Father Paul.

a. What differences are there between Teofilo's burial clothes and the priest's clothes?

b. What might be the significance, at the end of the funeral, of Father Paul "facing into a cold dry wind and squinting at the last sunlight" (lines 148–49), "while the faces of his parishioners were in shadow with the last warmth of the sun on their backs" (lines 150–51)?

c. What other contrasts did you notice?

3. In Laguna Pueblo culture, blue, red, yellow, and green are associated with the four points of the compass (for example, blue with the west and yellow with the east) as well as with corn, corn pollen, and other aspects of religious belief. In addition, sets of four are the standard, just as in Western culture, sets of three are common (for example, three witches in *Macbeth*). As you may have noticed, Silko has divided this story into four parts.

Using what you have learned from the story, as well as your knowledge of general culture, which of the following have a religious significance in the culture of the Laguna Pueblo? Which have a religious significance in Christian culture? Which have religious importance in both cultures?

> *corn meal and corn pollen; a lamb; holy water; rain water; a red blanket; the colors blue, yellow, red, and green; sets of three; sets of four; burying the dead*

M̲aking Connections

1. From what we see in this story, what rituals do Teofilo's people follow when a member of the tribe dies? What help does the tribe expect from someone who has died? In your culture, what customs are followed when someone dies? Are people who have died expected to help the living?

2. How much satisfaction is Father Paul getting from his life in the pueblo? If you could write him a letter, what might you say? Write for ten minutes without stopping to see what you can think of. Then compare your ideas with those of your classmates.

3. Either with the whole class or in groups of three, read the two scenes between Leon and Father Paul (lines 34–43 and 98–136) aloud. Each scene calls for a LEON, a FATHER PAUL, and a NARRATOR. What causes them to misunderstand each other?

4. Has there been a time when someone encouraged you to change your cultural or religious beliefs? Or, have you sometime tried to change someone else's deeply held beliefs? Who was involved? What was the situation? How did it end?

5. A misunderstanding between two people is important in both this story and Ernest Hemingway's "Hills Like White Elephants." However, in this story the misunderstanding concerns a death, while that in Hemingway's story concerns a potential birth. How else are the misunderstandings in the two stories different? In what ways are they similar?

6. To learn more about American Indian culture, consult a history text such as *Cycles of Conquest* (1962) by Edward H. Spicer; an anthropological study such as *The Pueblo Indians of North America* (1970) by Edward P. Dozier, who is an enrolled member of the Santa Clara, New Mexico, Pueblo; or the interviews with contempo-

rary Indian writers by Laura Coltelli (1990). Willa Cather's novel *Death Comes for the Archbishop* (1927) presents a deeply felt picture of the region from the point of view of two French missionary priests in the mid-1800s.

For a different approach, there are a number of excellent children's books. Among them are *Hawk, I'm Your Brother* (1976), about a young Mexican American, and *The Desert Is Theirs* (1975), both by Byrd Baylor with illustrations by Peter Parnall. These two Caldecott Award–winning books provide captivating and accurate depictions of Southwest desert life.

The Somebody

"A spray can has no heart. The letters come out very dead."

The Somebody

Danny Santiago
(1911–1988)

Reading "The Somebody," it seems clear that Danny Santiago must be a young, Mexican American author who grew up in Los Angeles. That's what reviewers said when Danny Santiago's first novel, *Famous All Over Town,* was published in 1984. In fact, the author was a man named Daniel James, a former screenwriter in his seventies who was the only son of a wealthy family from Kansas City. He was close to sixty when he wrote "The Somebody," which slowly developed into the novel. How did Dan James from Kansas City become Danny Santiago from Los Angeles?

Daniel James's grandfather (who was a cousin of the notorious outlaws Frank and Jesse James) became a wealthy man as an importer and seller of fine china in Kansas City. The business passed to his son, Daniel's father, a Yale graduate who wrote plays as a hobby and built a second home on the Pacific coast near Hollywood. Dan James also went to Yale, where he was the only member of the class of 1936 to major in classical Greek. After college, jobs in an Oklahoma oil field and as a traveling salesman for the family business gave Dan James his first glimpse of the lives of uneducated laborers and Depression-ruined middle-class families. Next he became an assistant to Charlie Chaplin, who was filming *The Great Dictator.* (James, six feet six inches tall, said years later that Chaplin "had a history of hiring tall, well-bred assistants who knew which fork to use.") As a member of Hollywood's newly-formed Screen Writers

Guild, James again saw how hard life was for the lower ranks of workers. To help improve working people's lives, he and many of his friends joined the Communist Party, though by 1948 he had dropped his membership as he became disenchanted with the Russian government.

In 1950, Wisconsin Senator Joseph McCarthy gained national attention by claiming that Communist agents in Hollywood were trying to overthrow the American government. After refusing to "cooperate" with McCarthy's investigating committee, Dan James and his wife found they could no longer work in Hollywood under their real names. (McCarthy was eventually censured by the Senate for making false claims, but only after he had ruined many people's careers.) Dan James wrote several monster pictures under an assumed name but he had lost confidence in himself as a writer. He also felt guilty about being able to live on inherited wealth.

James and his wife both spoke Spanish well and for some time they had been volunteer social workers in Eastside, a Los Angeles neighborhood of more than one and a half million Mexican Americans. They turned their energies to that project and became friendly with a dozen or more families. Gradually, Dan James began to write again, using the voice of his Chicano self and the Spanish version of his name. In 1968, he showed some of his stories to a younger friend who was a writer and who knew something about James's political past. The friend, John Gregory Dunne, sent the Danny Santiago stories to his literary agent, who soon placed them in national publications.*

One of the first published stories was "The Somebody," narrated by fourteen-year-old Chato Medina, a street-smart kid with an IQ of 135. "This is a big day in my life," Chato tells us, "because today I quit school and went to work as a writer." What kind of writer do you suppose he is going to be? Telling us of the adventures of his first day as a writer, Chato speaks of his home, his street, his school, the neighborhood playground, the juvenile court, the Boys' Club, and the business district near his home. How much security, understanding, and pleasure do you suppose he has found in each of those places? What disappointment or danger has he found in each?

* Much of the material in this introduction is from Dunne's splendid interview, "The Secret of Danny Santiago," *The New York Review of Books* (August 16, 1984).

Uncommon Words or Meanings

de ("Chato *de* Shamrock")—"of"; in traditional Spanish family names, the *de* is a sign of aristocracy.

an arsenal ("I still have our old *arsenal*")—a stockpile of guns or other weapons.

a tire iron ("There's *tire irons* . . .")—a steel bar with a flattened end used in changing the tire on an automobile.

a hot rod ("roars like a *hot rod* taking off") (slang) an automoblie that has been modified for greater speed and power.

a zip gun ("two *zip guns* we made")—a homemade "gun" that uses powerful rubber bands to shoot small pieces of lead.

a dump ("I'm leaving this *dump*!")—(slang) a poorly cared for, dirty place.

khakis ("put on my *khakis*")—slacks made of khaki, a sturdy light-brown cotton fabric.

Qué cute! ("everybody . . . says *'Qué cute!'*")—(a mixture of Spanish and English) "How cute!" "How adorable!"

to bawl (someone) out ("to *bawl* me *out* for not going to school")—(informal) to scold angrily.

to cut out ("So I *cut out*.")—(slang) to leave abruptly.

to pay a call ("wouldn't dare to *pay* any *calls* on Shamrock Street")—to come for a proper social visit, an old-fashioned term here used sarcastically.

S.P. Railroad ("the *S.P. Railroad* bought up the whole street")—the Southern Pacific Railroad.

to cruise ("So I *cruised* on down to Main Street ")—(slang) to move casually, with the idea of being noticed by others.

an Anglo ("real nice, for an *Anglo*")—Among Latinos, a white person who speaks English and is not of Latin descent.

Juvenile ("had me in *Juvenile* by mistake")—Short for "Juvenile Court," a court of law for offenders under a set age, sixteen in many states.

a dime store ("I slid into the *dime store*")—(informal) A place where only inexpensive merchandise is sold; originally, most prices were only five or ten cents—a nickel or a dime.

to help (one)self to ("*helped myself to* two boxes")—to take, rather than waiting to be served; here, to take without paying.

a spray can ("writing . . . with *spray cans*")—a pressurized can of paint.

a joint ("the Zócalo, which is a beer *joint*")—(slang) a cheap, disreputable bar.

Plymouth ("the *Plymouth* agency")—a medium-priced make of automobile.

to get a kick out of ("Everybody *got a kick out of* it.")—(slang) to be pleasantly surprised and amused by.

to whip ("she *whips* it behind her")—to move quickly or suddenly.

a sewer ("got to the first *sewer*")—an underground channel, with a metal grill opening onto the street, to carry off sewage or rainwater.

Beverly Hills ("We'd go to *Beverly Hills*")—the expensive residential area northwest of Los Angeles where many movie stars live.

The Somebody

This is Chato talking, Chato de Shamrock, from Eastside in old L.A., and I want you to know this is a big day in my life because today I quit school and went to work as a writer. I write on fences or buildings or anything that comes along. I
5   write my name, not the name I got from my father. I want no part of him. I write my gang name, Chato, which means Cat-face, because I have a flat nose like a cat. It's a Mexican word because that's what I am, a Mexican, and I'm not ashamed of it. I like that language, too. It's way better than English to say
10   what you mean. But German is the best. It's got a real rugged sound, and I'm going to learn to talk it someday.

After Chato I write "de Shamrock." That's the street where I live, and it's the name of the gang I belong to, but the others are all gone now. Their families had to move away, except
15   Gorilla is in jail and Blackie joined the navy because he liked swimming. But I still have our old arsenal. It's buried under the chickens and I dig it up when I get bored. There's tire irons and chains and pick handles with spikes and two zip guns we made but they don't shoot very straight.
20   In the good old days nobody cared to tangle with us. But now I'm the only one left.

Well, today started off like any other day. The toilet roars like a hot rod taking off. My father coughs and spits about nineteen times and hollers, "It's six-thirty." So I holler back,
25   "I'm quitting school." Things hit me like that—sudden.

"Don't you want to be a lawyer no more," he says in Span-ish, "and defend the Mexican people?"

My father thinks he is very funny, and next time I get an idea what I'm going to do in the world, he's sure not going to
30   hear about it.

"Don't you want to be a doctor," he says, "and cut off my leg for nothing when I ask you? How will you support me," he says, "when I retire? Or will you marry a rich old woman that owns a pool hall?"
35   "I'm leaving this dump! You'll never see me again!"

I hollered it at him, but he was already in the kitchen mak-ing a big noise with his coffee. I could be dead and he would-n't take me serious. So I laid there and waited for him to go off

to work. When I woke up again, it was way past eleven. So I
got out of bed and put on my khakis and my horsehide jacket
and combed myself very careful because already I had a feeling this was going to be a big day for me.

I had to wait for breakfast because the baby was sick and
throwing up milk on everything. There is always a baby vomiting in my house. When they're born, everybody comes over
and says "*Qué* cute!" but nobody passes any comments on the
dirty way babies act.

When my mother finally served me, I had to hold my
breath, she smelled so bad of babies. I don't like to look at her
anymore. Her legs got those dark blue rivers running all over
them. I kept waiting for her to bawl me out for not going to
school, but I guess she forgot or something. So I cut out.

Every time I go out my front door I have to cry for what
they've done to old Shamrock Street. It used to be so fine,
man, with solid homes on both sides. Then the S.P. Railroad
bought up the whole street, every house except my father's.
He's real stubborn, to give him credit. But what good did it do?
The wreckers came rolling in with their trucks and bulldozer.
You could hear the houses scream when they ripped apart. So
now Shamrock Street is just front walks that lead to a hole in
the ground. And Pelón's house and Blackie's are just stacks of
old boards waiting to get hauled away. I hope that never happens to your street, man.

My first stop was the front gate and there was that sign
again, a big S wrapped around a cross like a snake, which is
the mark of the Sierra Street gang, as everybody knows. I
rubbed it off, but tonight they'll put it back again. In the old
days they wouldn't dare to pay any calls on Shamrock Street,
but without your gang you're nobody. And one of these fine
days they're going to catch up with me in person and that will
be the end of Chato de Shamrock.

So I cruised on down to Main Street like a ghost in the
graveyard. Just to prove I'm alive, I wrote my name on the parking-lot fence at the corner. A lot of names you see in public
places are written very sloppy. Not me. I take my time. Like my
fifth-grade teacher used to say, "If others are going to see your
work, you owe it to yourself to do it right." Mrs. Cully was her
name and she was real nice, for an Anglo. My other teachers
were cops, all of them, but one time Mrs. Cully drove me home
when some guys were after me. I think she wanted to adopt me,

too, but she never said anything about it. I owe a lot to that lady, and especially my handwriting. You should see it, man—it's real smooth and mellow, and curvy like a girl in a bathing suit. Everybody says so. Except one time they had me in Juvenile by mistake and some doctor looked at my writing. He said it proved I had something wrong with me. That doctor was crazy, because I made him show me *his* writing and it was very ugly, like a barbed-wire fence with little chickens stuck on the points and all flapping their wings.

So anyway, I signed myself very clean and neat on that corner. And then I thought, Why not go look for a job someplace? But I was more in the mood to write my name, so I slid into the dime store and helped myself to two boxes of crayons and plenty of chalk. Some people lately have taken to writing their name with spray cans, but they'll get over it. A spray can has no heart. The letters come out very dead. Give me good old chalk any day. And so I cruised down Main, writing as I went, till a sudden question hit me. I wondered should I write more than my name. Should I write, "Chato is a fine guy," or "Chato is wanted by the police"? Things like that. But I decided no. Better to keep them guessing.

So I cut over to Forney Playground. It used to be Shamrock territory, but now the Sierra have taken over there like every-place else. Just to show them, I wrote on the tennis court and the swimming pool and the gym. I left a fine little trail of Chato de Shamrock in eight colors. Some places I used chalk, which works better on brick or plaster. But crayons are the thing for cement or anything smooth.

I'm telling you, I was pretty famous at the Forney by the time I cut out, and from there I continued my travels till a new idea hit me. You know how you put your name on something and that proves it belongs to you? Things like schoolbooks or gym shoes? So I thought, how about that now? And I put my name on the Triple A Market and on Morrie's Liquor Store and on the Zócalo, which is a beer joint. Then I cruised on up Broadway, getting rich. I took over a barber shop and a furni-ture store and the Plymouth agency. And the firehouse for laughs, and the phone company so I could call all my girlfriends and keep my dimes. And then there I was at Webster and Gar-cia's Funeral Home with the big white columns. At first I thought that might be bad luck, but then I said, Oh, well, we all got to die sometime. So I signed myself, and now I can eat good and live in style and have a big time all my life, and then kiss you all good-by and give myself the best funeral in L.A. for free.

125 And speaking of funerals, along came the Sierra guys right then, eight or twelve of them cruising down the street with that stupid walk which is their trademark. I ducked behind the hearse. Not that I'm a coward. Getting beat up doesn't bother me. What I hate is those blades. They're like a piece of ice cut-
130 ting into your belly. But the Sierra didn't see me and went on by. I couldn't hear what they were saying but I knew they had me on their mind. So I ducked into the Boys' Club, where they don't let anybody get you, no matter who you are. To pass the time I shot some baskets and played a little pool and watched
135 the television, but the story was boring, so it came to me, Why not write my name on the tube? Which I did with one of these squeaky pens. The cowboys sure looked fine with Chato de Shamrock pasted all over them. Everybody got a kick out of it. But of course up comes Mr. Calderon and makes me wipe it
140 off. They're always spying on you up there. And he takes me into his office and closes the door.

"Well," he says, "and how is the last of the dinosaurs?"

"What's that?" I ask him.

He shows me their picture in a book, giant lizards and real
145 ugly, worse than octopus, but they're all dead now, and he explains he called me that because of the Shamrocks. Then he goes into that voice with the church music in it and I look out the window.

"I know it's hard to lose your gang, Chato," he says, "but
150 this is your chance to make new friends and straighten your-self out. Why don't you start coming to Boys' Club more?"

"It's too boring," I tell him.

"What about school?"

"I can't go," I said. "They'll get me."

155 "The Sierra's forgotten you're alive," he tells me.

"Then how come they put their mark on my house every night?"

"Do they?"

He stares at me very hard. I hate those eyes of his. He
160 thinks he knows everything. And what is he? Just a Mexican like everybody else.

"Maybe you put that mark there yourself," he says. "To make yourself big. Just like you wrote on the television."

"That was my name! I like to write my name!"

165   "So do dogs," he says. "On every lamppost they come to."

    "You're a dog yourself," I told him, but I don't think he heard me. He just went on talking. Brother, how they love to talk up there! But I didn't bother to listen, and when he ran out of gas I left. From now on I'm scratching that Boys' Club off

170 my list.

    Out on the street it was beginning to get dark, but I could still follow my trail back toward Broadway. It felt good to see myself written everyplace, but at the Zócalo I stopped dead. Around my name there was this big red heart in lipstick and

175 somebody's initials. To tell the truth, I didn't know how to feel. In one way I was mad to see my name molested, especially if by some guy for laughs. But if it was a girl, that could be more or less interesting. And who ever heard of a guy carrying lipstick?

    A girl is what it turned out to be. I caught up with her at the

180 telephone building. There she is, standing in the shadows and drawing her heart around my name. She has a very pretty shape on her, too. I sneak up very quiet, thinking all kinds of crazy things. And my blood shoots around so fast it shakes me up and down all over. And then she turns around and it's only

185 Crusader Rabbit. That's what we called her since third grade, from the television show because of her big teeth in front.

    When she sees me, she takes off down the alley, but in twenty feet I catch her. I grab for the lipstick, but she whips it behind her. I reach around and try to pull her fingers open, but

190 her hand is sweaty and so is mine. And then she loses her balance and falls against some garbage cans, so I get the lipstick away from her very easy.

    "What right you got to my name?" I tell her. "I never gave you permission."

195   "You sign yourself real fine," she says.

    I knew that already.

    "Let's go writing together," she says.

    "The Sierra's after me."

    "I don't care," she says. "Come on, Chato—you and me can

200 have a lot of fun."

    She came up close and giggled. She put her hand on my hand that had the lipstick in it. And you know what? I'm ashamed to say I almost told her yes. It would be a change to go writing with a girl. We could talk there in the dark. We could

205 decide on the best places. And her handwriting wasn't too bad

either. But then I remembered my reputation. Somebody would be sure to see us, and then they'd be laughing at me all over Eastside. So I pulled my hand away and told her off.

"Run along, Crusader," I told her. "I don't want no partners and especially you."

"Who you calling Crusader?" she yelled. "You ugly squash-nose punk!"

She called me everything. And spit in my face but missed. I didn't argue. I just cut out. And when I got to the first sewer, I threw away her lipstick. Then I drifted over to Broadway, which is a good street for writing because a lot of people pass by there. I don't mind crowds. The way I write, nobody notices till I'm finished, and I can smell a cop for half a mile.

You know me, I hate to brag but my work on Broadway was the best I've ever done in all my life. Under the street lamp my name shone out like solid gold. I stood to one side and checked the people as they walked past and inspected it. With some you can't tell just how they feel, but with others it rings out like a cash register. There was one man. He got out of a brand new Cadillac to buy a paper and when he saw my name he smiled. He was the age to be my father. I bet he'd give me a job if I asked him. I bet he'd take me to his home and to his office in the morning. Pretty soon I'd be sitting at my own desk and signing my name on letters and checks and things. But I would never buy a Cadillac. They burn too much gas.

Later a girl came by. She was around eighteen, I think, with green eyes. Her face was so pretty I didn't dare look at her shape. Do you want me to go crazy? That girl stopped and really studied my name like she fell in love with it. She wanted to know me, I could tell. She wanted to take my hand and we'd go off together just holding hands and nothing dirty. We'd go to Beverly Hills and nobody would look at us in the wrong way. I almost said "Hello" to that girl, and "How do you like my writing?" but not quite.

So here I am, standing on the corner of Broadway and Bailey with my chalk all gone and just one crayon left and it's an ugly brown. My fingers are too cold to write, but that's nothing, man, nothing, because I just had a vision. I saw the Sincere Truth in flashing lights. I don't need to be a movie star or light-weight boxing king. All I need is plenty of chalk and I'll be famous wherever there's a wall to write on. The Sierra will try

to stop me, and the cops and everybody, but I'll be like a ghost, mysterious, and all they'll ever know of me is just my name, signed the way I always sign it, **CHATO DE SHAMROCK,**
250 with rays shooting out like from the Holy Cross.

[1970]

Understanding the Story

1. In this story, we learn about Chato from what he tells us both directly and indirectly.

   a. [T]hat's what I am, a Mexican, and I'm not ashamed of it. (line 8)

   Compare that statement with Chato's later comment (lines 160–61) about Mr. Calderon: "And what is he? Just a Mexican like everybody else."

   b. . . . without your gang you're nobody. (line 69)

   What has become of Chato's gang?

   c. What other remarks tell the reader something that isn't said directly?

2. From the evidence in the two following examples what kind of relationship does Chato have with his parents?

   a. "Don't you want to be a lawyer no more," he says in Spanish, "and defend the Mexican people?" (lines 26–27)

   b. When my mother finally served me, I had to hold my breath, she smelled so bad of babies. I don't like to look at her anymore. (lines 48–50)

3. Chato's interest in other people is shown by his exclamation, "I hope that never happens to your street, man" (lines 62–63). What other good qualities does he have? What passages in the text provide evidence for your answer?

4. How well does Chato get along with the counselor at the Boys' Club? For example, what does Mr. Calderon mean

by calling Chato "the last of the dinosaurs" (line 142), and what does Chato mean when he says that Mr. Calderon started speaking in "that voice with the church music in it" (line 147)? What does Mr. Calderon imply by his question "Do they?" (line 158)?

5. Twice Chato is disrespectful to an older man. First, he tells his father that their home is a "dump" and that he, Chato, is leaving for good (line 35). Later, he calls Mr. Calderon a dog (line 166). Why do you suppose neither of the older men responds?

6. Chato refers frequently to death. For example, he says of his father, "I could be dead and he wouldn't take me serious" (lines 37–38) and of the Sierra Street Gang, "one of these fine days they're going to catch up with me in person and that will be the end of Chato de Shamrock" (lines 69–71).

   Where else does he refer to death? Do you think it is realistic for him to worry about dying?

7. What are the stages in the comic "love scene" (lines 179–215) between Chato and Crusader Rabbit? For example, how does she declare her affection? What is their first physical contact? How does she respond to Chato's verbal challenge? Why is he tempted by her suggestion that they team up? Why does he finally reject her? How realistic is this scene?

8. When Chato finally explains the way he signs his name, how does that help us to understand the reactions of the passers-by? Throughout the story, Chato has referred to himself as "a ghost"? In what sense *is* he a ghost? How is that related to the title of the story?

Developing a Way with Words

1. Often when a story is told in the first-person, by a narrator who says "I did this, and I did that," the reader is expected to see things that the narrator does not. Also,

the narrator, to quote one reader, "sometimes makes himself look good at the expense of the truth. " To see how "The Somebody" illustrates this literary convention, examine the following four types of statement and then find additional examples for each one.

a. *Factually true:* I write my gang name, Chato, which means Catface, because I have a flat nose like a cat. (lines 6–7).

Crusader Rabbit is less tactful (lines 211–12) when she calls him an "ugly squash-nose punk."

b. *Humorous exaggeration:* The toilet roars like a hot rod taking off. (lines 22–23)

c. *Reflection of wishes or dreams:* I think she [Mrs. Cully] wanted to adopt me, too, but she never said anything about it. (lines 80–81)

d. *Bragging to gain attention or status:* I'm telling you, I was pretty famous at the Forney by the time I cut out, ... (lines 109–10)

2. "Without your gang you're nobody," says Chato. Read the following poem by the nineteenth-century American poet Emily Dickinson, then discuss the three questions that follow.

I'm Nobody! Who are you?

I'm Nobody! Who are you?
Are you—Nobody—too?
Then there's a pair of us!
Don't tell! they'd banish us—
    you know!
How dreary—to be—Somebody!
    How public—like a Frog —
To tell your name—the
    livelong June—
To an admiring Bog!

banish—exile, force to leave.
dreary—dull, tiring.

livelong—whole, entire.
bog—soft, water-soaked land.

    a. Do you think Chato would recognize the sense of being "Nobody" that the speaker of this poem expresses? Why or why not?

    b. If you think he would, do you think he would be willing to admit his feeling to the poem's speaker? Why or why not?

    c. Do you think the poem's speaker would agree with Chato that writing your name on a wall is a good way to gain recognition? Why or why not?

Making Connections

1. How typical are the teenagers in this story? How do they help and hurt each other?

2. Can you think of a time when you wanted to be recognized for something? What did you do to achieve recognition? Did your effort succeed? Why or why not? What did you learn from the experience?

3. In Spanish-speaking cultures, *machismo*—being a man—is a vitally important concept. (The term has entered the English language in the adjective *macho*.) Some of the elements of *machismo* are having the respect of others, being brave, and never giving in to the desires of a woman. How do the events in Chato's day reflect this concept?

4. Why do you think young people join gangs? Why are they considered a problem in the many cities where they exist?

5. Chato speaks of giving himself "the best funeral in L.A. for free" (line 124). How do you think Chato would respond to this poem by the twentieth-century American poet Mari Evans? In what sense is the poem's speaker a

"rebel"? Why does the speaker expect that a lot of people will come to his or her funeral?

The Rebel

When I
die
I'm sure
I will have a
Big
Funeral . . .
Curiosity
seekers . . .
coming to see
if I
am really
Dead . . .
or just
trying to make
Trouble . . . .

6. The wandering hero is a universal figure in literature. In Western literature, the most famous example is Odysseus. In the *Odyssey,* the Greek poet Homer tells the story of Odysseus's wandering as he tries to return home to his faithful wife and young son after the Trojan War. Because the gods are angry with him, Odysseus must sail over the Aegean and Mediterranean seas for twenty years, encountering an array of giants, witches, and other dangers before his final success.

   Some thirty centuries later, the Irish writer James Joyce presented a parallel version of the story in his novel *Ulysses,* the Latin version of the hero's name. In Joyce's novel, however, the hero is an ordinary man, the action takes place on a single day in Dublin, the characters are human, the wife is unfaithful, and the "son" is a young man whom the hero meets for the first time that day.

   In "The Somebody," Danny Santiago keeps the idea of wandering during a single day but reduces the range from a single city to a single neighborhood and uses a son, rather than a father, as the main character.

Find a brief description of the adventures in the *Odyssey*. (One good source is Edith Hamilton's classic book *Mythology* 1942.) What parallels can be found in "The Somebody"? For example, could Mrs. Cully be seen as the goddess Athena (who helped Odysseus when the other gods were against him) and Crusader Rabbit as a siren? What other stories do you know of a wandering hero?

Japanese Hamlet

"'Some day I'll be the ranking Shakespearean actor,' he said."

Japanese Hamlet

Toshio Mori
(1910–1980)

Toshio Mori was a twentieth-century pioneer in Asian American literature, one who memorably recorded the experience of the seventh and eighth generations of Asian American citizens. He was the first Japanese American short story writer to be published in the U.S. and was one of the first published Asian American writers.

Mori's father had left Japan in the 1890s to prepare a new life for his wife and two sons in the United States, first working on a sugar plantation in Hawaii and then establishing a nursery in Oakland, California, where he grew plants and trees. In 1907, the American law changed to allow Japanese immigrants to bring wives from Japan, so long as the women didn't work. After Mrs. Mori joined her husband, Toshio and his younger brother were born. Then the two older sons were allowed to come from Japan. (For years, Toshio thought that his older brother was his father.) As a youngster, Mori was torn between a love of baseball and a love of reading. When his mother advised him to do less reading and more writing, Mori realized that he really wanted to be a writer and that he wanted to counteract the Asian stereotypes that he found in popular American fiction. Like the central character in "Japanese Hamlet," Mori knew that writers and other artists rarely make much money, so he accepted the idea of earning a living by working in the family nursery. His short story collection *Yokohama, California* was scheduled for publication in 1941, but the project was halted in response to the Japanese attack on Pearl Harbor and the book did not appear until 1949. During World War II, the Mori family, along with almost all other American citizens of Japanese ancestry, were regarded as potential spies and were forced to move to an internment center in a remote part of the American West. (Those Japanese Americans who volunteered for the American Army were sent to fight in Europe; one of Mori's older brothers served in Italy, where he received battle wounds that left him permanently paralyzed.)

When Mori's book appeared, the popular author William Saroyan (represented in volume 1) praised him as "a natural born writer." Some critics' complaints that Mori's English wasn't always perfect were gracefully answered by his friend and fellow-writer Hisaye Yamamoto (also represented in volume 1): "I think Toshio, just as I, was trying to use the very best English of which he was capable, and we have both run aground on occasion. Probably this was because we both spent the pre-kindergarten years speaking only Japanese, and, in such cases, *Sprachgefühl* [a feeling for the spoken language] is hard to come by."*

"Japanese Hamlet" first appeared in *Pacific Citizen,* the weekly publication of the Japanese-American Citizens League, in 1939. The story is set in Piedmont, a wealthy suburb of San Francisco. It seems to begin in the middle of a conversation, for the first six sentences refer to an unidentified "he," who proves to be the narrator's friend Tom Fukunaga. Many years before, Tom had defied the expectations of the Japanese American community in order to pursue a dream. As the narrator's tale unfolds, we learn about Tom's dream and the narrator's part in it. From the title, can you guess what the dream was? The conflict between dreams and reality is a theme in many works of literature. Perhaps it is also true of the lives of people whom you know.

* From Yamamoto's introduction to Mori's second short story collection, *The Chauvinist and Other Stories* (1979), which is also the source of the Saroyan quote later in "Making Connections."

U ncommon Words or Meanings

Hamlet (title)—*The Tragedy of Hamlet, Prince of Denmark* is the best-known of William Shakespeare's plays. Because of his father's sudden death, Hamlet has returned home from his studies. His mother has quickly married her late husband's brother, who has named himself king. A ghost appears to Hamlet, saying "I am your father's spirit, murdered by my own brother. You must avenge my death." Hamlet promises to do so. But then he worries that perhaps the ghost was the devil in disguise. What if his uncle/stepfather is innocent? Hamlet alternates between uncertainty and impulsive action that finally leads to many deaths, including his own.

a Piedmont home ("a schoolboy in a *Piedmont home*")—Piedmont is a well-to-do suburb of San Francisco. Tom was probably working as a gardener for an upper-middle-class family.

room and board ("pay for *room and board*")—a place to sleep and three meals a day.

carfare ("pay for . . . *carfare*")—the cost of daily public transportation, e.g., by trolley car.

the blues ("Have you got *the blues*?")—(informal) a feeling of sadness.

Macbeth ("That night we took up *Macbeth.*)—In *The Tragedy of Macbeth,* three witches tell Macbeth, a Scottish noble who is also a brave and victorious general, that he will one day become king of Scotland. Urged on by his ambitious wife, Lady Macbeth, he murders the present king and other innocent people to make the prophecy come true. In the end, however, Macbeth is defeated by his own ambition.

ranking ("the *ranking* Shakespearean actor")—leading, most important.

a forte ("Hamlet is my *forte.*")—something in which a person excels, a strong point.

He used to come to the house and ask me to hear him recite. Each time he handed me a volume of *The Complete Works of William Shakespeare*. He never forgot to do that. He wanted me to sit in front of him, open the book, and follow
5   him as he recited his lines. I did willingly. There was little for me to do in the evenings so when Tom Fukunaga came over I was ready to help out almost any time. And as his love for Shakespeare's plays grew with the years he did not want anything else in the world but to be a Shakespearean actor.
10   Tom Fukunaga was a schoolboy in a Piedmont home. He had been one since his freshman days in high school. When he was thirty-one he was still a schoolboy. Nobody knew his age but he and the relatives. Every time his relatives came to the city they put up a roar and said he was a good-for-nothing
15   loafer and ought to be ashamed of himself for being a schoolboy at this age.

"I am not loafing," he told his relatives. "I am studying very hard."

One of his uncles came often to the city to see him. He
20   tried a number of times to persuade Tom to quit stage hopes and schoolboy attitude. "Your parents have already disowned you. Come to your senses," he said. "You should go out and earn a man's salary. You are alone now. Pretty soon even your relatives will drop you."

25   "That's all right," Tom Fukunaga said. He kept shaking his head until his uncle went away.

When Tom Fukunaga came over to the house he used to tell me about his parents and relatives in the country. He told me in particular about the uncle who kept coming back to
30   warn and persuade him. Tom said he really was sorry for Uncle Bill to take the trouble to see him.

"Why don't you work for someone in the daytime and study at night?" I said to Tom.

"I cannot be bothered with such a change at this time," he
35   said. "Besides, I get five dollars a week plus room and board. That is enough for me. If I should go out and work for someone I would have to pay for room and board besides carfare so

I would not be richer. And even if I should save a little more it would not help me to become a better Shakespearean actor."

When we came down to the business of recitation there was no recess. Tom Fukunaga wanted none of it. He would place a cup of water before him and never touch it. "Tonight we'll begin with Hamlet," he said many times during the years. Hamlet was his favorite play. When he talked about Shakespeare to anyone he began by mentioning Hamlet. He played parts in other plays but always he came back to Hamlet. This was his special role, the role which would establish him in Shakespearean history.

There were moments when I was afraid that Tom's energy and time were wasted and I helped along to waste it. We were miles away from the stage world. Tom Fukunaga had not seen a backstage. He was just as far from the stagedoor in his thirties as he was in his high school days. Sometimes as I sat holding Shakespeare's book and listening to Tom I must have looked worried and discouraged.

"Come on, come on!" he said. "Have you got the blues?"

One day I told him the truth: I was afraid we were not getting anywhere, that perhaps we were attempting the impossible. "If you could contact the stage people it might help," I said. "Otherwise we are wasting our lives."

"I don't think so," Tom said. "I am improving every day. That is what counts. Our time will come later."

That night we took up Macbeth. He went through his parts smoothly. This made him feel good. "Some day I'll be the ranking Shakespearean actor," he said.

Sometimes I told him I liked best to hear him recite the sonnets. I thought he was better with the sonnets than in the parts of Macbeth or Hamlet.

"I'd much rather hear you recite the sonnets, Tom." I said.

"Perhaps you like his sonnets best of all," he said. "Hamlet is my forte. I know I am at my best playing Hamlet."

For a year Tom Fukunaga did not miss a week coming to the house. Each time he brought a copy of Shakespeare's complete works and asked me to hear him say the lines. For better or worse, he was not a bit downhearted. He still had no contact with the stage people. He did not talk about his uncle who kept coming back urging him to quit. I found out later that his uncle did not come to see him any more.

In the meantime Tom stayed at the Piedmont home as a
80 schoolboy. He accepted his five dollars a week just as he had
done years ago when he was a freshman at Piedmont High.
This fact did not bother Tom at all when I mentioned it to him.
"What are you worrying for?" he said. "I know I am taking
chances. I went into this with my eyes open so don't worry."
85   But I could not get over worrying about Tom Fukunaga's
chances. Every time he came over I felt bad for he was wasting his life and for the fact that I was mixed in it. Several times
I told him to go somewhere and find a job. He laughed. He kept
coming to the house and asked me to sit and hear him recite
90 Hamlet.
        The longer I came to know Tom the more I wished to see
him well off in business or with a job. I got so I could not stand
his coming to the house and asking me to sit while he recited.
I began to dread his presence in the house as if his figure
95 reminded me of my part in the mock play that his life was, and
the prominence that my house and attention played.
        One night I became desperate. "That book is destroying
you, Tom. Why don't you give this up for awhile?"
        He looked at me curiously without a word. He recited sev-
100 eral pages and left early that evening.
        Tom did not come to the house again. I guess it got so that
Tom could not stand me any more than his uncle and parents.
When he quit coming I felt bad. I knew he could never abandon
his ambition. I was equally sure that Tom would never rank
105 with the great Shakespearean actors, but I could not forget his
simple persistence.
        One day, years later, I saw him on the Piedmont car at
Fourteenth and Broadway. He was sitting with his head buried
in a book and I was sure it was a copy of Shakespeare's. For a
110 moment he looked up and stared at me as if I were a stranger.
Then his face broke into a smile and he raised his hand. I
waved back eagerly.
        "How are you, Tom?" I shouted.
        He waved his hand politely again but did not get off, and
115 the car started up Broadway.

[1939]

Understanding the Story

1. How old was Tom when the narrator first became involved with him? What was Tom's one ambition in life? Why did he regularly visit the narrator?

2. What can a reader infer (understand from what is suggested, rather than stated directly) about the narrator? For example, is the narrator a man or a woman? Is the narrator an educated person? Is the narrator, like Tom, a member of the Japanese American community in Piedmont or a nearby town? How do you know?

3. For a time, one of Tom's uncles came often to "warn and persuade him" (line 30) to give up the idea of a career in acting.

   a. Why do you suppose Tom's family disapproved of his ambition?

   b. How do you imagine they expected Tom to respond to their concerns? Why?

   c. Why do you think Tom ignored his uncle's advice?

4. What reasons did Tom give for not wanting a paying job? Were his reasons just excuses for laziness, or did he really believe in his chosen life's work? Why do you think so?

5. Hamlet is recognized as the most complex of Shakespeare's characters; it is a part that many great actors have played.

   a. Why do you suppose Tom saw Hamlet as his "special role" (line 47)—his "forte" (line 71)?

   b. From what you know about Hamlet, can you see any similarities between him and Tom? What differences do you see?

   c. Why do you think the narrator preferred hearing Tom recite the sonnets to hearing him recite the speeches of Hamlet or Macbeth?

6. Tom was also attracted by the role of Macbeth, a man of action who is destroyed by his own ambition. Is that at all like Tom? What are some ways in which Tom and Macbeth are unlike?

7. How are Tom's attitude and situation shown in the following comments?

   a. "I am improving every day. That is what counts." (lines 61–62)

   Would you agree that improvement is just as important as ultimate success?

   b. "Our time will come later." (line 62)

   Whose time? Time for what?

   c. "I know I am taking chances. I went into this with my eyes open so don't worry." (lines 83–84).

   What chances is he taking? What does he mean by "with my eyes open"?

8. The narrator says, "There were moments when I was afraid that Tom's energy and time were wasted and I helped along to waste it" (lines 49–50).

   a. What does that comment show about the narrator's attitude toward Tom's dream?

   b. What other comments in the story show how the narrator felt?

   c. How would you explain the narrator's feelings?

9. When the narrator first "told [Tom] to go somewhere and find a job" (line 88), Tom only laughed and kept coming to recite, but when the narrator later suggested that he "give this up for awhile" (line 98), Tom stopped coming. Why do you think Tom reacted that way? Why was he willing to abandon his contact with his parents, relatives, and friends rather than give up his dream?

10. How do you think the narrator felt when he saw Tom again years later (lines 108–109), "sitting with his head buried in a book"? Why do you think Tom didn't get off the trolley car when he finally noticed his friend?

Developing a Way with Words

Here are three examples of Shakespeare's work that Tom surely recited from memory. Choose one to discuss in terms of what it means and what Tom might have felt about it. Then, to better understand Tom's experience, practice reading aloud the excerpt you have chosen until you can recite it, just as Tom did.

1. In Sonnet 18, the speaker asks, "Shall I compare thee [you] to a summer's day?" but then says, no, you are even lovelier than that. Moreover, "thy [your] eternal summer shall not fade" because even after death, you will live on in this poem. Here is the sonnet's conclusion:

> So long as men can breathe,or eyes can see,
> So long lives this, and this gives life to thee.

2. At the beginning of his most famous soliloquy, Hamlet is torn between thought and action. He asks himself if it is more noble for him, as a prince, to simply accept life's hardships bravely, or if he should fight against his troubles, even if that struggle brings him peace only through his own death.

> To be, or not to be—that is the question,
> Whether 'tis nobler in the mind to suffer
> The slings and arrows of outrageous fortune,
> Or to take arms against a sea of troubles
> And by opposing end them.
> (Act 3, scene 1, lines 56–60)

'tis—it is.
outrageous—cruel.
arms—weapons.
a sea—endless turmoil.

3. Shakespeare was an actor as well as a playwright. In both *Hamlet* and *Macbeth,* he compares the world to a theater and human life to a drama on the stage. At the end of *Macbeth,* as his hard-won power is slipping away from him, Macbeth learns from a servant that his wife has died suddenly (one interpretation is that she has killed herself). Macbeth's response is this:

> Out, out, brief candle!
> Life's but a walking shadow,a poor player
> That struts and frets his hour upon the stage
> And then is heard no more. It is a tale,
> Told by an idiot, full of sound and fury,
> Signifying nothing.
> (Act 5, scene 5, lines 23–28)

brief candle—the spark of life.
life's but—"life is only."
player—actor.
struts and frets—moves and speaks (his part in a play).
It—here, life.

Making Connections

1. If you had been one of Tom's relatives, what advice would you have given him? Working in small groups, write and then present either a scene in which Tom tells his father that he wants to be a Shakespearean actor or the scene of Tom's uncle trying to reason with him.

2. Hisaye Yamamoto quotes the author William Saroyan, who encouraged Mori in his work, as saying that Mori "sees through a human being to the strange, comical, melancholy truth that changes a fool to a great solemn hero."

a. How well does that description fit this story?

b. At the beginning of the story, in what way does Tom seem to be a fool?

c. By the end of the story, in what sense is he a hero?

d. Is there a "strange, comical, melancholy truth" that helps us to see that change?

3. Do you know someone who, like Tom, has faced a conflict between a longing for self-expression and family pressure to earn a living, or someone who wanted to achieve a seemingly impossible goal? If so, how was that person's conflict resolved? If you know someone who is facing that problem now, how do you think the conflict will end?

4. Compare Tom in "Japanese Hamlet" and Chato in "The Somebody" in their goals and the problems they face in achieving them. If you have read William Saroyan's story "The Summer of the Beautiful White Horse" in volume 1 of this text, what similarities can you see between the Armenian American characters in that story and Tom Fukunaga and the narrator in "Japanese Hamlet"? What differences are there?

5. How important is it that Tom is Japanese? Have members of other ethnic minorities faced the same kinds of problems? Have you ever felt, as the narrator does, that because of your family background or because of another factor that you cannot change, such as your height or your gender, you may have difficulty succeeding? If so, how have you dealt with the challenge?

6. In 1977, the Pan Asian Repertory Theatre was established to provide professional opportunities for Asian American actors and playwrights. They perform in New York and other American cities. If you live in the United States, write to them at 423 W. 46th Street, New York, New York 10036 to find out what projects they have undertaken and if they are presenting any plays in your part of the country this year. On the West Coast, you

might contact the East West Players, 4424 Santa Monica Boulevard, Los Angeles, CA 90029 to inquire about their activities.

7. For an introduction to other Asian American writing, see *Aiieeeee!,* edited by Frank Chin and others (1975), and Elaine H. Kim, *Asian American Literature: An Introduction to the Writings and Their Social Context* (1982).

Secrets

" . . . my life had

started to seem

like too much

trouble."

Secrets

Judy Troy
(born 1951)

Judy Troy sets her stories in many different parts of the country, reflecting her experience living in the South, Southwest, and West. The plot of "Secrets," which first appeared in *The New Yorker* magazine in 1992, is completely fictional. "On an emotional level, however," Troy affirms, "in the way Jean [the narrator] feels and in the things she notices and responds to, the story is very autobiographical."

As a child, Troy enjoyed both writing and acting. When she reached adolescence, she found that she was too self-conscious to perform but she did continue writing poems and stories in private. "I liked being able to become someone else, to create a different life from the one I was living, and I also liked being able to say what was secret within myself." Although she was twenty-six before she felt at all confident about her writing, Troy feels that the self-doubt was valuable. "I was able to be very critical of my own work," she says. "I never thought writing well would be easy, and I never minded rewriting." As a teacher of creative writing (at Indiana University, the University of Missouri-Columbia, and presently at Auburn University in Alabama), Troy helps her students to discover what every writer comes to learn—that writing a story is a much more intuitive than intellectual activity. "I have to get to know my characters," Troy explains, "to understand what they would realistically think and say. I don't always know what will happen, or how a story will end, until I write it. Then I have to revise it over and over again until it says what I want it to."

The characters in Troy's stories are small-town, blue-collar Americans struggling to find security, and perhaps some meaning, in their lives. "Secrets," the third of the four "Florida Stories" in *Mourning Doves* (1993), is narrated by a teenage girl. The girl's father has tried, and failed at, a succession of jobs in Indiana. Deciding that he should go into business with a relative in Key West, he packs up the family to move there. But by the time they reach Jacksonville, in northern Florida, they are out of money. "Secrets" tells some of what happens next. The narrator's voice seems rather flat—she doesn't show much emotion in telling about her life and she reports actions without analyzing people's motives. Yet this surface simplicity is deceptive. Along with the events of the twenty-four hour period from a Sunday evening to Monday evening, we learn about the family's history and also develop a sense of what the next few years may bring. What are the "secrets" of the title? Are they secrets that people have kept from other people? Could they be secrets that people have kept from themselves?

Uncommon Words or Meanings

Interstate 95 ("a small house near *Interstate 95*")—a highway running from Maine to Florida.

a cookout ("invited us to a *cookout*")—a picnic at which some foods are cooked outdoors.

heavy ("I was tall and too *heavy*.")—overweight, fat.

limp ("the rest of him *limp* on the floor")—with the muscles completely relaxed.

a utility room ("meant to be a small *utility room*")—a room for household appliances such as machines for washing and drying clothes.

a spitball ("shot *spitballs* at the red-haired boy")—(informal) a small piece of paper crumpled up and moistened with saliva (spit).

A Separate Peace ("a sentence from *A Separate Peace*")—a 1959 novel by John Knowles about a boy's coming of age in a New England boarding school.

to mark off ("*marking off* our names as we walked in")—here, to make a note that someone is present.

to shoot baskets from the freethrow line ("went to the basketball court and *shot baskets from the freethrow line*")—to throw a basketball through a hoop from a marked spot eight feet away.

a study hall ("went to the library for *study hall*")—in high school, a class period when students work quietly on their individual assignments.

a touchdown ("I made a *touchdown*")—in football, six points scored by carrying the ball over the opponents' goal line or throwing it to a teammate behind the goal line.

to cancel out ("something nice that would *cancel out* her angry words")—to make up for, neutralize, remove the impact of.

Secrets

My father died in 1966, from a fall at a construction site where he was working, in Jacksonville, Florida. I was thirteen, and my brothers, Eddie and Lee, were eleven and eight. We had just moved from an apartment into a small house near Interstate 95, but our real home was South Bend, Indiana. We had only been in Florida for eight months. Both sets of grandparents wanted us to return to Indiana.

"They think I'm helpless," my mother said, "which makes me angry."

We were in the car on a Sunday night, two weeks after my father's funeral, driving home from the beach. My mother was working as a secretary at my brothers' elementary school, and her friends from work had invited us to a cookout. My mother said the cookout was to cheer us up. But, once her friends had got the fire going, they talked about how sad they felt for us. "What kind of food did your father like?" my mother's friend Grace Nolan asked us.

"Meat," Eddie said, "and not many kinds of vegetables."

Grace Nolan started to cry.

"Well, he liked potatoes, too," Lee told her.

"So," my mother said to us now, in the car, "I told your grandparents we'd be staying here."

"Good," Eddie said, from the back seat. Of the three of us—Eddie and Lee and me—he was the one who had made the most friends.

"I'm not sure I want to stay," I told my mother. "Or if Lee does." Lee was asleep, next to Eddie, with his head and shoulders on the seat and the rest of him limp on the floor.

"Lee wants to stay, Jean," my mother said. "I already know that." She pulled up in front of our house. It was ten o'clock, and we had forgotten to leave on any lights.

"Wake up, Lee," my mother said. She got out of the car and opened the back door and gently shook him. Sometimes he slept so soundly that it was impossible to wake him up. He opened his eyes for a moment and looked at the dark house.

"Why isn't Dad home yet?" he asked. My mother picked him up and carried him inside. He and Eddie were small for their ages, whereas I was tall and too heavy. I watched my mother put Lee into bed. Eddie lay down on his own bed, against the opposite wall, and fell asleep with his clothes on.

My mother and I went into the kitchen. Spread out over the table were letters from the construction company my father had worked for, and forms from its insurance company. We were supposed to receive twenty-five thousand dollars, and my mother was planning to use this money to buy the house we were in, which would allow us to live on the salary she made. The problem was that there had been people around, when the accident happened, who said the fall had been my father's own fault, and not the fault of the construction company. So there was a chance the insurance company might not pay us. My mother was worried about this, and now she sat down at the table and began to fill out the forms.

I went into my room, next to the kitchen, which was really meant to be a small utility room. My father had painted it yellow and put in carpeting for me. I changed into my nightgown and got into bed. Every night since my father died, I had been unable to fall asleep. During the day I didn't cry, and it didn't upset me to hear about things my father had said or done. But as soon as I was almost asleep, memories would come into my mind that made our situation seem real to me. I stayed awake all night, it seemed to me, listening to my mother in the kitchen and to the distant noise of the cars on the highway.

In the morning, my mother made me get up and get ready for school. My brothers and I had stayed home for a week after my father died, and then my mother allowed me to stay home for an additional week. I told her I didn't want to talk to people at school yet, but the truth was also that I had got used to staying home—to being able to wear my nightgown all day if I wanted to, or lie in bed all morning, reading a book. I didn't want to go back to living my life, because my life had started to seem like too much trouble. Each small thing, like brushing my teeth or putting on knee-socks, now made me tired. I felt I had to do fewer things each morning, in order to save energy for some more important thing I might have to do in the afternoon.

After I ate breakfast, I walked to the end of our block and waited for the bus with Nancy Dyer, who was in my class. It was November, and she was wearing a blue corduroy jumper her mother had made. She had brought over my assignments, for

the two weeks I had been home, and on the bus we went over
them. I made corrections according to the answers she remembered from class. "You did real well," she said when we were finished. "But then, you're smarter than I am to begin with."

"That's not true," I told her. "I just do more homework."

"That's what I mean," she said. She had her eyes on her boyfriend, who was getting on the bus. He was a thin boy, with black hair. He sat in front of us. He ignored her and took out a piece of notebook paper and shot spitballs at a red-haired boy across the aisle.

"He's mad at me all the time now," Nancy whispered. "I don't know why."

She had tears in her eyes, and I looked away and watched the trees flashing past in the window. In the reflection, I could see that three people on the bus were looking at me—the red-haired boy, and two girls in the seat in front of him. When I first got on the bus, one of these girls had said, "There was an announcement in school about your dad."

"I know," I said. "Nancy told me."

"I can't believe that happened to you," she said, and whispered something that I couldn't hear to the other girl. Now, as I turned away from the window and looked across the aisle, the red-haired boy smiled at me and was about to say something when he was hit in the forehead by a spitball.

When we got to school, I went to my locker to put away my sweater, and then I went to science and algebra and history. In each class, the teacher took me aside and talked to me about my father, and two or three other people spoke to me about him as well. The boys, especially, wanted to know exactly what happened. "Did he step off the beam by accident," one boy asked, "or was there something he tripped over?"

"I think he tripped," I told him.

"Wow," the boy said. "I can just picture that."

During lunch, the group of girls I sat with stopped talking to each other when I walked up. "You can sit here, in the middle," Roberta Price said. Everyone moved over, and Carla Norris unwrapped my straw and put it in my milk. "We wondered when you were coming back," Roberta said. "The principal thought maybe last week."

"I decided to wait until today," I told her. We began to eat. Most of us had bought hot lunches. We all had mothers who were either too busy in the mornings to make us sandwiches or who felt we were old enough how to make them ourselves. Carla was the one exception. Her mother not only made her a sandwich but put a note in with her lunch every day.

"Here it is," Carla said. She unfolded a small piece of yel-
low paper. "Good luck on your geography quiz," she read out loud. "Your father and I are very proud of you." She and every-body else at the table looked down at their food.

"That's better than the one where she told you to wash off your mascara," I said, after a silence.
"It sure is," Roberta said quickly. "That one was sickening."

I had English class afterward, during fourth period. My Eng-lish teacher, Mr. Thompson, was sitting at his desk when I walked in. I went to my seat and listened to a boy standing next to Mr. Thompson's desk talk to him about commas. "I don't
think we need them," the boy said. "Periods are good enough."

Other people were coming into the room, and Mr. Thomp-son went up to the blackboard and wrote down a sentence from *A Separate Peace*. The sentence was, "Perhaps I was stopped by that level of feeling, deeper than thought, which
contains the truth." After the bell rang, he stepped back from the board and asked, "What, exactly, does this sentence mean?"

Four people he called on said they didn't know. The fifth person said, "I think it means a feeling you keep to yourself."

"Why wouldn't you want anyone to know?" Mr. Thompson
asked.

"Because it's a secret," someone else said.

"Maybe it's a secret you keep from yourself," a girl in the back row said. "Maybe people don't want to know their own secrets."
"That doesn't make sense," a boy said.

"A lot of things don't make sense," Mr. Thompson told him, "but they're still true." He gave us an assignment, which we were to do in class, and then he sat on the radiator and watched us work. "Don't forget to use commas," he told us.
After class, I went downstairs to the girls' locker room to change my clothes for gym. Our teacher was already there, marking off our names as we walked in. She talked to me about my father, and then a girl I knew from another class said, "I don't know what I would do if my father died, even though I
hate him."

We all went out to the basketball court and shot baskets from the free-throw line. After gym, I went to the library for study hall, and then I met Nancy in front of my locker, and we walked out to the school bus. Her boyfriend, who got on the bus a few minutes after we did, sat down four rows ahead of us. He spent the whole bus ride talking loudly to a small, blond girl.

"Sometimes people try to hurt you just to see if they can do it," Nancy said.

"You don't know that for sure," I told her.

"Yes, I do," she said. "I've done it to people myself."

We got off at our block and stood for a moment at the corner before we each went home. The air was so still that the traffic from the highway seemed louder than usual. "I guess I don't need to talk to you about feeling sad," Nancy said. "I forgot for a minute."

"It's different with me," I told her. "It's not something you feel every second."

I walked across the neighbors' yard and into our own; I put Lee's bike in the shed and went into the house through the kitchen door. My mother was standing in Lee's doorway, and I heard Lee say, "I got an A in spelling. Dad gave me fifty cents last time."

My mother gave Lee two quarters, and then she walked past me into the kitchen, opened the kitchen door, and sat outside on our steps. I went out and sat beside her. "Did Dad really give Lee fifty cents?" she asked me.

"I thought it was a quarter," I told her, "but I might be remembering it wrong." She held my hand, and we watched a squirrel race around the shed.

"Would you give me a hug, honey?" she asked. I put my arms around her. In the past year, I had grown a lot, and now I was bigger than she was; when I hugged her, I was able to put my arms all the way around her.

"I wish I'd stop growing," I told her.

"You'll be tall, like Dad was," she said. "Someday you'll appreciate it." She stood up and walked down into the yard. She was still dressed in her work clothes—a skirt and blouse and high heels—and her shoes were invisible in the long grass. No one had mowed the yard since my father had died. "The lawn will have to be Eddie's job now," my mother said. "You and Lee can do the raking." She looked up toward the clatter of a woodpecker in our sweetgum tree. "I'll find a gas station that will change the oil in the car, and then I'll teach myself to do the other things Dad did."

205   "That seems like a lot," I told her.

"I know it does, honey." She sat back down beside me and pulled up weeds that were growing out of the cracks in the steps. I looked around at the yard and the house—at the patches of bare ground under the trees, the peeling paint
210 around the windows, and all the small holes in the screens—and thought that it would take an army of men to fix everything that was broken.

My mother and I went inside to peel potatoes. At six o'clock, when Eddie came home from playing football with his
215 friends, we all had supper in the kitchen.

"I made a touchdown today," Eddie said.

"Well, good for you," my mother said, "I wish I could have seen it." She had eaten quickly, and she put her plate in the sink and drank a cup of instant coffee while she watched us finish.

220   Afterward, I cleared the table and washed the dishes. I forgot that it was Eddie's turn, and he didn't remind me until I was done. He and Lee were sitting on the floor in the living room, with Lee's toy soldiers all around them. They were watching television with my mother. I came in the room and said, "I
225 don't feel like watching TV."

"Who cares?" Eddie asked.

"We all care," my mother said sharply. "We're a family, even without Dad. We care what happens to each other." The way she spoke and the look on her face reminded me of my father, of the
230 times he'd lost his temper with us. Eddie and Lee looked surprised, and then, a second later, there were tears on their faces.

I was crying, too, because my mother had started to cry. But I wasn't upset about what Eddie had said or because my mother had got angry. I startled myself by feeling almost glad.
235 It seemed to me that all of a sudden our lives were ordinary again, except that my father wasn't there, and I felt like I was paying attention after being lost in a daydream, or like I was opening my eyes after seeing how long I could keep them closed. When my mother started to speak, I hoped she would-
240 n't say something nice that would cancel out her angry words.

But what she said was, "O.K. Pick up these toys. Then we're going to turn off the television and go to bed."

245 It was only seven-thirty, but we went into our rooms. I didn't bother to put on my nightgown. I took off my clothes and got into bed in my underwear, and, even though it was early, I didn't have my same trouble falling asleep. I knew now that my father was dead and that we would live our lives without him, and I fell asleep right away, so that for a while I could not know these things.

[1993]

Understanding the Story

1. In each of the following statements, Jean uses very calm language to present emotionally powerful information. What is she saying indirectly, rather than directly?

   a. . . . our real home was South Bend, Indiana. (line 5)

   b. . . . there had been people around, when the accident happened, who said that the fall had been my father's own fault, and not the fault of the construction company. (lines 47–50)

2. How did the family members differ in their reactions to the husband/father's death? For example, why didn't the mother want to move back to South Bend? How did the boys react? Why didn't Jean want to go back to school? What might explain some of the differences?

3. People often feel awkward talking about someone who has just died. Sometimes the person who has come to offer comfort needs to be comforted. (That reversal of expectation and actuality is an example of irony.)

   a. At the cookout, why did Grace Nolan start to cry (line 19)? What did Lee think the reason was? How did he try to comfort her?

   b. In the school cafeteria, why did all the girls look down at their food (lines 126–27) after Carla read aloud the note from her mother? Who broke the silence?

c. When Nancy said (lines 173–75), "I guess I don't need to talk to you about feeling sad. I forgot for a minute," how did Jean put her friend at ease?

4. What might explain why, after eight months in Jacksonville, Jean still felt like an outsider?

   a. What factors suggest why she hadn't made a lot of friends? Why might it have been easier for her brother Eddie?

   b. How does the mini-drama of Nancy's trouble with her boyfriend (lines 84–90) relate to Jean's situation?

5. What is the underlying meaning of Nancy's exchange with Jean about which of them is smarter (lines 81–84) and Nancy's later statement about hurting people (lines 167–70)?

6. What caused the family quarrel at the end of the story? What did the mother say that was important for all the family? Why do you think Jean felt relieved after her mother got angry? Do you think the other family members felt the same way? Why or why not?

7. Look back at the classroom discussion of the sentence from *A Separate Peace* (lines 138–52). What was Jean's secret? How did she become aware of it? (This could also be a topic for writing.)

8. What other secrets appear in the story? Which of them were ones that people were keeping from themselves? (This could also be a topic for writing.)

Developing a Way with Words

1. Many Americans send a short letter of condolence—a sympathy note—to a friend when someone in the friend's family has died. A sympathy note typically says that you have heard the news, that you are very sorry that the person has died, and that you extend your sympathy to all the family. It is also nice to offer encouragement to the person you are writing to.

Imagine that you are a friend of Jean's parents from South Bend, and that you have just heard about the father's death. Use the following suggestions—modifying the contents as you choose—to write a three-paragraph sympathy note to Jean's mother. (You will need to invent a name for the mother.) *Paragraph one:* Say that you have just heard the sad news and that you offer your deepest sympathy to her and the children. *Paragraph two:* Say what a fine man/good friend/good husband and father her husband was (make up a name for him too) and tell her something you remember about him that made you like him (make up the memory). *Paragraph three:* Either assure Jean's mother that you know she will do well in raising the children on her own, or say you hope she will return to South Bend so that the children's grandparents can help her to raise them.

2. Consider the statement of the boy in Jean's English class that commas are unnecessary or could be replaced by periods (lines 134–35). Of the fifty-eight paragraphs in this story, only one has no commas. Which one is it?

   In small groups, choose another paragraph and examine the use of commas in it. Read your chosen paragraph aloud, with and without the commas. How is it different when the commas are left out? Could they be replaced with periods?

M aking Connections

1. Judy Troy has said of the story, "Jean, in her own way, feels like an outsider, a foreigner. She probably even felt that way in Indiana, for it's a feeling shared by all sensitive teenagers. For Jean, the feeling is heightened by the death of her father, which sets her apart from her peers, and even from herself." Do you agree with Troy that all sensitive teenagers feel like outsiders, like foreigners? Do you agree that the death of a parent sets someone apart from his or her peers (others of the same age and social class) and even from himself or herself?

2. Have you had an experience, like that in the story, of someone close to you dying when you were a child? If so, what aspects of the story do you recognize as being similar to your experience? What aspects are different?

3. Using the following questions as a stimulus, try to remember your experiences in school during a particular year. Find one or more aspects of that time to discuss with the whole class, or in a small group, or in an essay.

   a. Were you an insider (like Nancy) or an outsider (like Jean)? Can you describe a particular incident to illustrate how being in one category or the other affected your life?

   b. In your school, were most of the students usually kind to each other? Did the boys and girls differ in their willingness to be kind to others? What might explain the situation in your school?

   c. Do you have a particular memory of someone who was a good friend—or a bad friend—to you in school?

   d. During that year, did you have a disappointment in love like Nancy's? If so, how was experience like and unlike hers?

4. "Maybe people don't want to know their own secrets," says one of the girls in Jean's English class. (lines 148–49)

   a. Do you think that statement is true? Do you agree that people often keep secrets from themselves?

   b. What examples—in real life or in fiction—do you know of people not wanting to know their own secrets, of people keeping secrets from themselves?

   c. Sandra Cisneros, the author of "No Speak English" in volume 1 of this series, urges her students to write about whatever is "so taboo you can't even think about it." Do you have a secret that you would be willing to write about? If so, write a short paper on it.

5. "Writing was both an escape into and from myself,"
   Judy Troy says. "And I now realize that writing is like
   acting for self-conscious or shy people: in both profes-
   sions you get to become someone else." Have you ever
   wanted to be either an actor or a writer? Why or why
   not? What is your present career goal? What appeals to
   you about the career path you are now considering or
   have chosen?

The Orphaned Swimming Pool

"True, late

splashes and

excited guffaws

did often keep

Mrs. Chace

awake. . . "

The Orphaned
Swimming Pool

John Updike
(born 1932)

Achronicler of contemporary middle-class and upper-middle-class American life, John Updike is the author of thirteen novels, nine collections of short stories, four children's books, and one play, as well as poetry, essays and criticism. How did such a writer develop from, as Updike has written of himself in *Self-Consciousness* (1989), "a very average little boy, and furthermore a boy who loved the average, the daily, the safely hidden"?

Updike was born in Shillington, a small town in eastern Pennsylvania, in 1932. His father was a high school math teacher who had previously been a telephone cable-splicer ("a telephone lineman" is mentioned in "The Orphaned Swimming Pool"). His parents and grandparents, like many Americans, had lost most of their money during the Depression. Nevertheless, Updike's mother, an unpublished writer, encouraged her son to plan a future in the arts—drawing or writing—rather than in a safe, ordinary job. Two other factors also influenced the unusual development of the "average little boy." The first factor was a pair of physical problems—a chronic skin disease and a stutter—that made Updike self-conscious about both his body and his speech. The second factor was his high intelligence, which enabled Updike to earn high grades in school, as well as a full scholarship to Harvard University and a one-year post-graduate fellowship to Oxford University.

At Harvard, Updike majored in English but wrote short stories only when they were required for a class, being much more interested in drawing cartoons and writing light verse. Yet the first story Updike wrote after graduating in 1954 was accepted by *The New Yorker,* and he worked as a staff writer there for a year when he returned from Oxford. In 1957, seeking a climate that would help him to control his skin problem, Updike moved to the Boston suburbs and became a full-time writer. There he has devoted his happiest hours to preparing words for print, "words as smooth in their arrangement and flow as repeated revision could make them."

"The voice of fiction speaks in images," Updike reminds us, noting that he finds his own fictional voice "when the images come abundantly, and interweave to make a continuous music." For "The Orphaned Swimming Pool," these images are based on the details of suburban American life. The story shows his characteristic use of brand names—for example, Triscuits (a salty wheat cracker), Agitrol (a chemical used to control algae), and Off! (a bug spray/insect repellent)—in creating a realistic setting. It also illustrates Updike's continuing interest in "the animating force of sexual desire behind polite appearances." What is the connection between sexual desire and a swimming pool? And what can the title mean? An orphan is a child who has lost both parents. How can a suburban swimming pool be "orphaned"?

Uncommon Words or Meanings

dissolution ("Marriages, like chemical unions, release upon *dissolution* packets of energy")—decomposition into fragments or parts; termination of a formal or legal bond or contract.

bonding ("the energy locked up in their *bonding*")—the force that holds atoms together; when the bond is broken, energy (motion, heat, or light) is released.

to go mad ("the dog *goes mad*")—to become infected with rabies (a dog); to become insane.

to score ("the Turners had *scored* again")—to make a point in a contest.

to hold court ("would *hold court* all day")—to entertain visitors, as a queen receives courtiers.

a solicitation ("stuffing . . . pornography *solicitations* into the mailbox")—(1) a request made using persuasion; (2) an offer of sexual services. Both meanings apply here.

an au-pair girl ("Swiss *au-pair girls*")—a young woman who lives with a family and looks after the children in exchange for room and board.

an honor system ("an *honor system* shoebox containing change")—an informal agreement that, without supervision, people will follow a set of rules.

Darien ("softball team from *Darien*")—a very fashionable Connecticut suburb of New York.

Hartford ("archery champion of *Hartford*")—an unfashionable city in northern Connecticut.

Good Intentions ("rock group called the *Good Intentions*")—from the proverbial expression "The road to hell is paved with good intentions."

Aly Khan ("an ex-mistress of *Aly Khan*")—a Pakistani prince known as a playboy and sportsman in his youth; Pakistani ambassador to the United Nations, 1958–60.

lavender-haired ("the *lavender-haired* mother-in-law")—with white hair tinted a purplish-blue.

Nixon ("a *Nixon* adviser")—Richard M. Nixon, American president, 1969–74.

a parkway ("killed the next day on the Merritt *Parkway*")—a highway on which no trucks or commercial vehicles are allowed.

a Maoist ("a student *Maoist*")—a follower of Mao Zedong, the primary Chinese Communist organizer and theoretician from the 1920s to his death in 1979.

Wesleyan ("from *Wesleyan*")—a fashionable private university in western Connecticut.

beaux ("The few lingering babysitters and *beaux*")—plural form of *beau,* a boyfriend.

ticklish ("The settlement was at a ticklish stage")—delicate, easy to upset.

The Orphaned Swimming Pool

Marriages, like chemical unions, release upon dissolution packets of the energy locked up in their bonding. There is the piano no one wants, the cocker spaniel no one can take care of. Shelves of books suddenly stand revealed as burdensomely dated and unlikely to be reread; indeed, it is difficult to remember who read them in the first place. And what of those old skis in the attic? Or the doll house waiting to be repaired in the basement? The piano goes out of tune, the dog goes mad. The summer that the Turners got their divorce, their swimming pool had neither a master nor a mistress, though the sun beat down day after day, and a state of drought was declared in Connecticut.

It was a young pool, only two years old, of the fragile type fashioned by laying a plastic liner within a carefully carved hole in the ground. The Turners' side yard looked infernal while it was being done; one bulldozer sank into the mud and had to be pulled free by another. But by midsummer the new grass was sprouting, the encircling flagstones were in place, the blue plastic tinted the water a heavenly blue, and it had to be admitted that the Turners had scored again. They were always a little in advance of their friends. He was a tall, hairy-backed man with long arms, and a nose flattened by football, and a sullen look of too much blood; she was a fine-boned blonde with dry blue eyes and lips usually held parted and crinkled as if about to ask a worrisome, or whimsical, question. They had never seemed happier, nor their marriage healthier, than those two summers. They grew brown and supple and smooth with swimming. Ted would begin his day with a swim, before dressing to catch the train, and Linda would hold court all day amid crowds of wet matrons and children, and Ted would return from work to find a poolside cocktail party in progress, and the couple would end their day at midnight, when their friends had finally left, by swimming nude, before bed. What ecstasy! In darkness the water felt mild as milk and buoyant as helium, and the swimmers became giants, gliding from side to side in a single languorous stroke.

The next May, the pool was filled as usual, and the usual after-school gangs of mothers and children gathered, but Linda, unlike her, stayed indoors. She could be heard within the house, moving from room to room, but she no longer

40   emerged, as in the other summers, with a cheerful tray of ice
      and brace of bottles, and Triscuits and lemonade for the chil-
      dren. Their friends felt less comfortable about appearing, tow-
      els in hand, at the Turners' on weekends. Though Linda had
      lost some weight and looked elegant, and Ted was cumber-
45   somely jovial, they gave off the faint, sleepless, awkward-mak-
      ing aroma of a couple in trouble. Then, the day after school
      was out, Linda fled with the children to her parents in Ohio.
      Ted stayed nights in the city, and the pool was deserted.
      Though the pump that ran the water through the filter contin-
50   ued to mutter in the lilacs, the cerulean pool grew cloudy. The
      bodies of dead horseflies and wasps dotted the still surface. A
      speckled plastic ball drifted into a corner beside the diving
      board and stayed there. The grass between the flagstones grew
      lank. On the glass-topped poolside table, a spray can of Off!
55   had lost its pressure and a gin and tonic glass held a sere mint
      leaf. The pool looked desolate and haunted, like a stagnant
      jungle spring; it looked poisonous and ashamed. The postman,
      stuffing overdue notices and pornography solicitations into
      the mailbox, averted his eyes from the side yard politely.
60   Some June weekends, Ted sneaked out from the city. Fam-
      ilies driving to church glimpsed him dolefully sprinkling chem-
      ical substances into the pool. He looked pale and thin. He
      instructed Roscoe Chace, his neighbor on the left, how to
      switch on the pump and change the filter, and how much chlo-
65   rine and Algitrol should be added weekly. He explained he
      would not be able to make it out every weekend—as if the dis-
      tance that for years he had traveled twice each day, gliding in
      and out of New York, had become an impossibly steep climb
      back into the past. Linda, he confided vaguely, had left her par-
70   ents in Akron and was visiting her sister in Minneapolis. As the
      shock of the Turners' joint disappearance wore off, their pool
      seemed less haunted and forbidding. The Murtaugh children—
      the Murtaughs, a rowdy, numerous family, were the Turners'
      right-hand neighbors—began to use it, without supervision. So
75   Linda's old friends, with their children, began to show up, "to
      keep the Murtaughs from drowning each other." For if any-
      thing were to happen to a Murtaugh, the poor Turners (the
      adjective had become automatic) would be sued for every-
      thing, right when they could least afford it. It became, then, a
80   kind of duty, a test of loyalty, to use the pool.

July was the hottest in twenty-seven years. People brought their own lawn furniture over in station wagons and set it up. Teenage offspring and Swiss *au-pair* girls were established as lifeguards. A nylon rope with flotation corks, meant to divide
85   the wading end from the diving end of the pool, was found coiled in the garage and reinstalled. Agnes Kleefeld contributed an old refrigerator, which was wired to an outlet above Ted's basement workbench and used to store ice, quinine water, and soft drinks. An honor system shoebox contain-
90   ing change appeared beside it; a little lost-and-found—an array of forgotten sunglasses, flippers, towels, lotions, paperbacks, shirts, even underwear—materialized on the Turners' side steps. When people, that July, said, "Meet you at the pool," they did not mean the public pool past the shopping center, or the
95   country-club pool beside the first tee. They meant the Turners'. Restrictions on admission were difficult to enforce tactfully. A visiting Methodist bishop, two Taiwanese economists, an entire girls' softball team from Darien, an eminent Canadian poet, the archery champion of Hartford, the six members of a
100 black rock group called the Good Intentions, an ex-mistress of Aly Khan, the lavender-haired mother-in-law of a Nixon adviser not quite of Cabinet rank, an infant of six weeks, a man who was killed the next day on the Merritt Parkway, a Filipino who could stay on the pool bottom for eighty seconds, two Texans
105 who kept cigars in their mouths and hats on their heads, three telephone linemen, four expatriate Czechs, a student Maoist from Wesleyan, and the postman all swam, as guests, in the Turners' pool, though not all at once. After the daytime crowd ebbed, and the shoebox was put back in the refrigerator, and
110 the last *au-pair* girl took the last goose-fleshed, wrinkled child shivering home to supper, there was a tide of evening activity, trysts (Mrs. Kleefeld and the Nicholson boy, most notoriously) and what some called, overdramatically, orgies. True, late splashes and excited guffaws did often keep Mrs. Chace
115 awake, and the Murtaugh children spent hours at their attic window with binoculars. And there was the evidence of the lost underwear.

One Saturday early in August, the morning arrivals found an unknown car with New York plates parked in the garage.
120 But cars of all sorts were so common—the parking tangle frequently extended into the road—that nothing much was

thought of it, even when someone noticed that the bedroom windows upstairs were open. And nothing came of it, except that around suppertime, in the lull before the evening crowds began to arrive in force, Ted and an unknown woman, of the same physical type as Linda but brunette, swiftly exited from the kitchen door, got into the car, and drove back to New York. The few lingering babysitters and beaux thus unwittingly glimpsed the root of the divorce. The two lovers had been trapped inside the house all day; Ted was fearful of the legal consequences of their being seen by anyone who might write and tell Linda. The settlement was at a ticklish stage; nothing less than terror of Linda's lawyers would have led Ted to suppress his indignation at seeing, from behind the window screen, his private pool turned public carnival. For long thereafter, though in the end he did not marry the woman, he remembered that day when they lived together like fugitives in a cave, feeding on love and ice water, tiptoeing barefoot to the depleted cupboards, which they, arriving late last night, had hoped to stock in the morning, not foreseeing the onslaught of interlopers that would pin them in. Her hair, he remembered, had tickled his shoulders as she crouched behind him at the window, and through the angry pounding of his own blood he had felt her slim body breathless with the attempt not to giggle.

August drew in, with cloudy days. Children grew bored with swimming. Roscoe Chace went on vacation to Italy; the pump broke down, and no one repaired it. Dead dragonflies accumulated on the surface of the pool. Small deluded toads hopped in and swam around hopelessly. Linda at last returned. From Minneapolis she had gone on to Idaho for six weeks, to be divorced. She and the children had burnt faces from riding and hiking; her lips looked drier and more quizzical than ever, still seeking to frame that troubling question. She stood at the window, in the house that already seemed to lack its furniture, at the same side window where the lovers had crouched, and gazed at the deserted pool. The grass around it was green from splashing, save where a long-lying towel had smothered a rectangle and left it brown. Aluminum furniture she didn't recognize lay strewn and broken. She counted a dozen bottles beneath the glass-topped table. The nylon divider had parted, and its two halves floated independently. The blue plastic

beneath the colorless water tried to make a cheerful, other-
worldly statement, but Linda saw that the pool in truth had no
bottom, it held bottomless loss, it was one huge blue tear.
165 Thank God no one had drowned in it. Except her. She saw that
she could never live here again. In September the place was
sold to a family with toddling infants, who for safety's sake
have not only drained the pool but have sealed it over with
iron pipes and a heavy mesh, and put warning signs around, as
170 around a chained dog.

[1970]

Understanding the Story

1. "Upon dissolution," the narrator says, both chemical
   unions and marriages release energy that had been
   "locked up in their bonding" (lines 1–2). That is, when
   either chemical or social bonds are broken, energy is
   released. According to the examples in the first paragraph of the story, what kinds of energy are released
   when a marriage ends in divorce?

2. What details in the second paragraph of the story establish that the Turners are part of the American upper-middle class?

3. How, when the Turners were gone for the summer, did
   their swimming pool become a center of neighborhood
   activity? How did the neighbors justify using the pool?
   What did the neighbors need to do to feel that everything was in order?

4. In every culture, people who fit in are seen to be "the
   same" as everyone else in their group—the same, for
   example, in age, income, religion, appearance, and
   opinion. In Updike's humorous catalogue of people who
   swam in the Turners' pool (lines 96–108), how is each
   person or group "different"—different, that is, from the
   Turners and their neighbors?

5. What picture does the story present of the sex lives of the American suburban upper-middle class in the 1960s?

6. What are the ironies (the differences between what could be or was expected and what actually happened) of the weekend when Ted came back to the house? For example, why weren't he and his mistress recognized when they arrived at the house? Why couldn't they enjoy a swim in the pool? What was the difference in their reactions to the situation of being trapped inside the house?

7. Linda's question is referred to twice—at the beginning of the story as "a worrisome, or whimsical, question" (lines 24–25) and the end of the story as "that troubling question" (line 153); but she never asks the question. What do you suppose it was?

Developing a Way with Words

Each of the seven paragraphs in the story illustrates the break-up—the dissolution—of a marriage through its effect on the divorcing couple's swimming pool. Using words from the story, complete the following chart. (The first paragraph has been done as an example.) Then answer the three questions based on the chart.

Analysis by Paragraph

Time period covered	Description of Pool
¶ 1 "The summer the Turners got their divorce"	"their swimming pool had neither master nor mistress"

(Now do the same for paragraphs 2–7.)

1. What time span does the story cover?

2. In which paragraphs is the pool described as a living thing? (The literary term for this is "personification.")

3. In which paragraphs is the pool described as being pleasant? In which paragraphs is it described as being unpleasant or potentially dangerous?

M aking Connections

1. What does the pool symbolize in the story? Why do you think Updike chose to focus on it, rather than on the children or one of the parents, in discussing the effects of the divorce? From your experience, what effects of a divorce has Updike chosen not to mention in this story?

2. Given Ted's fear of discovery, why do you think he risked bringing his mistress to the house?

3. What aspects of Ted and Linda's world does Updike invite the reader to laugh at? Are the Turners and their friends people that you would like to meet? Why or why not?

4. How is the Turners' experience of divorce unique to people of their nationality and social class? In other social groups that you are familiar with, is divorce permitted? Do you think that a reader who is not part of the Turners' world can understand the story? Participate in it emotionally? Why or why not?

5. Compare the lives of the people in this story to the lives of the people in other stories you have read in this book. For example, thinking of "Secrets" by Judy Troy, which people in this story had secrets? What were the secrets? Thinking of Danny Santiago's story, do you suppose Linda felt like a "somebody" at the beginning of the story? What about at the end?

The Sojourner

"Certainly his love

for his ex-wife was

long since past.

So why the

unhinged body,

the shaken

mind?"

The Sojourner

Carson McCullers
(1917–1967)

Born and raised in Georgia, Carson McCullers lived for most of her adult life in or near New York City. She was a promising pianist in her childhood but realized as a young adult that her real talent was for writing. McCullers became a literary celebrity with her first novel, *The Heart Is a Lonely Hunter* (1940), published when she was only twenty-three. Though chronic ill-health limited her output, she completed three other novels (including *The Member of the Wedding*, 1946, which was later turned into a successful play and film), twenty short stories, two plays, and a children's book, as well as poetry and essays.

All of McCullers's short stories deal in one way or another with rejection or unrequited love, and many of them have characters who share some of McCullers's personal history. In "The Sojourner," the title character, John Ferris, is a Southerner who, like McCullers, has chosen to live outside the South as an adult. Ferris also shares personality traits with Reeves McCullers, whom the author married twice and who ultimately committed suicide in Paris.

"The Sojourner" invites the reader into the sophisticated world of well-to-do Southerners now living in other parts of the world. John Ferris works in Paris as an international newspaper correspondent. He has lived for brief periods of time—"sojourned," as he says—in various European capitals, speaks French, and has had a series of mistresses since his divorce eight years earlier. He is undaunted by a twelve-hour (pre-jet) transatlantic flight, but he has been shaken by the death of his father, who had had a year of treatment at the prestigious Johns Hopkins Medical Center in Baltimore, a hospital well-known for its treatment of cancer, a disease not spoken of openly at the time the story was written.

Ferris's ex-wife lives with her second husband and their two children in a fashionable part of New York City. Their live-in housekeeper can easily prepare a Southern-style company meal on short notice. While the adults talk over cocktails, the housekeeper feeds the children and then serves dinner. The wife, like McCullers herself, is an amateur pianist who enjoys playing for others and is fond of the intricate music of Johann Sebastian Bach. After an early dinner, the couple can arrive at the theater for an 8:30 performance. What problems could there possibly be in such comfortable lives? And what connection do their lives have with those of less-privileged people?

Uncommon Words or Meanings

a sojourner (title)—someone who stays for a brief time in each of a series of places.

Ferris ("John *Ferris* awoke")—a family name, reminiscent of "Ferris Wheel," a large upright, rotating wheel with suspended seats in which passengers ride for amusement.

matinal ("This feeling, submerged by *matinal* necessities")—part of the early hours of the day.

a belly bulge ("his body was spare except for an incipient *belly bulge*")—a softening of the stomach ("belly") muscles, as well as excess stomach fat.

to unravel ("*unraveled* his filial devotion")—(literally) to cause the threads of a piece of fabric to pull apart.

a B.T.O. ("a *B.T.O.* in television")—(slang) Big Time Operator, an important person.

to hit the skids ("*hit the skids* after the war")—(slang) to become headed for failure.

transience ("a sense of hazard, of *transience*")—the state or quality of being **transient,** that is, of (1) lasting only a brief time; (2) passing through on the way from one place to another. Both meanings apply here.

carriage ("Elizabeth had a 'beautiful *carriage*'")—one's manner of holding the head and body.

an anodyne ("the *anodyne* of time")—something that can relieve or soothe mental distress.

a carving set ("sent a *carving set* when he received an announcement of her wedding")—a heavy knife and fork used by the host to cut and serve meat at the dining table.

a marquee ("a building with a *marquee* and a doorman")—a canopy from the front door to the street, a sign of elegance for an apartment building.

lumbering ("a *lumbering*, red-haired man")—moving heavily.

a Martini ("a cocktail shaker of *Martinis*")—the most fashionable before-dinner drink at the time of the story; made of three parts gin and one part dry vermouth.

to prime ("With the *priming* drinks they pumped up conversation.")—to pour water into (a pump) to start its action.

crêpe de Chine ("a pale pink *crêpe de Chine* frock")—literally, China crêpe, a silk fabric.

to smock ("a pale pink crêpe de Chine frock, *smocked* around the yoke with rose")—to embroider with a decorative stitch that gathers the cloth tightly, used on expensive babies' clothes.

an expatriate ("be an *expatriate*")—a person living outside of his or her own country.

an amiability ("one of her *amiabilities*")—a good-natured, pleasant quality.

a prelude ("a Bach *prelude* and fugue")—an independent piece of moderate length that precedes a fugue.

a fugue ("a Bach prelude and *fugue*")—a musical form in which the same melody is repeated by different instruments or "voices," playing first one after the other, then in an overlapping fashion that blends them into a grand melodious whole.

a catalyst ("*catalyst* for this tumultuous anarchy")—something that causes a change.

anarchy ("this tumultuous *anarchy*")—disorder, confusion.

Miz ("*Miz* Bailey, dinner is out on the table now.")—"Mrs." in the Black English of the period.

an improvisation ("the *improvisation* of human existence")—something improvised, done as needed, without previous preparation.

to know ("I first *knew* Jeannine last autumn")—here, to meet; Ferris is unconsciously translating directly from French.

a White Russian ("married to a *White Russian*")—a Russian who recognizes the former czarist government as the only legal government of Russia.

the guignol ("go to the *guignol*")—a comic puppet show for children, presented outdoors in warm weather.

the Tuileries ("go to *the Tuileries*")—a public park in the center of Paris.

an air ("the melody, the unfinished *air*")—a melody or tune.

a cadence ("The *cadence,* some related tones")—the rhythm and pacing of a musical work.

to jettison ("the load of memory *jettisoned*")—(literally) to throw something overboard to lighten a ship in distress. (In this sentence, the load seems to jettison itself.)

Monsieur Jean ("'*Monsieur Jean,*' the child said")—"Mr. John"; in French, a polite way for a child to address an adult who is a close family friend.

protean ("an emotion as *protean* as his love")—readily assuming a different form or character (like the Greek god Proteus, who could change his shape at will).

The Sojourner

The twilight border between sleep and waking was a Roman one this morning: splashing fountains and arched, narrow streets, the golden lavish city of blossoms and age-soft stone. Sometimes in this semi-consciousness he sojourned again in Paris, or war German rubble, or Swiss skiing and a snow hotel. Sometimes, also, in a fallow Georgia field at hunting dawn. Rome it was this morning in the yearless regions of dreams.

John Ferris awoke in a room in a New York hotel. He had the feeling that something unpleasant was awaiting him— what it was, he did not know. The feeling, submerged by matinal necessities, lingered even after he had dressed and gone downstairs. It was a cloudless autumn day and the pale sunlight sliced between the pastel skyscrapers. Ferris went into the next-door drugstore and sat at the end booth next to the window glass that overlooked the sidewalk. He ordered an American breakfast with scrambled eggs and sausage.

Ferris had come from Paris to his father's funeral which had taken place the week before in his home town in Georgia. The shock of death had made him aware of youth already passed. His hair was already receding and the veins in his now naked temples were pulsing and prominent and his body was spare except for an incipient belly bulge. Ferris had loved his father and the bond between them had once been extraordinarily close—but the years had somehow unraveled this filial devotion; the death, expected for a long time, had left him with an unforeseen dismay. He had stayed as long as possible to be near his mother and brothers at home. His plane for Paris was to leave the next morning.

Ferris pulled out his address book to verify a number. He turned the pages with growing attentiveness. Names and addresses from New York, the capitals of Europe, a few faint ones from his home state in the South. Faded, printed names, sprawled drunken ones. Betty Wills: a random love, married now. Charlie Williams: wounded in the Hürtgen Forest, unheard of since. Grand old Williams—did he live or die? Don Walker: a B.T.O., in television, getting rich. Henry Green: hit the skids after the war, in a sanitarium now, they say. Cozie Hall: he had heard that she was dead. Heedless, laughing Cozie—it was strange to think that she too, silly girl, could die. As Ferris closed the address book, he suffered a sense of hazard, transience, almost of fear.

It was then that his body jerked suddenly. He was staring out of the window when there, on the sidewalk, passing by, was his ex-wife. Elizabeth passed quite close to him, walking slowly. He could not understand the wild quiver of his heart, nor the following sense of recklessness and grace that lingered after she was gone.

Quickly Ferris paid his check and rushed out to the sidewalk. Elizabeth stood on the corner waiting to cross Fifth Avenue. He hurried toward her meaning to speak, but the lights changed and she crossed the street before he reached her. Ferris followed. On the other side he could easily have overtaken her, but he found himself lagging unaccountably. Her fair brown hair was plainly rolled, and as he watched her Ferris recalled that once his father had remarked that Elizabeth had a "beautiful carriage." She turned at the next corner and Ferris followed, although by now his intention to overtake her had disappeared. Ferris questioned the bodily disturbance that the sight of Elizabeth aroused in him, the dampness of his hands, the hard heartstrokes.

It was eight years since Ferris had last seen his ex-wife. He knew that long ago she had married again. And there were children. During recent years he had seldom thought of her. But at first, after the divorce, the loss had almost destroyed him. Then after the anodyne of time, he had loved again, and then again. Jeannine, she was now. Certainly his love for his ex-wife was long since past. So why the unhinged body, the shaken mind? He knew only that his clouded heart was oddly dissonant with the sunny, candid autumn day. Ferris wheeled suddenly, and walking with long strides, almost running, hurried back to the hotel.

Ferris poured himself a drink, although it was not yet eleven o'clock. He sprawled out in an armchair like a man exhausted, nursing his glass of bourbon and water. He had a full day ahead of him as he was leaving by plane the next morning for Paris. He checked over his obligations: take luggage to Air France, lunch with his boss, buy shoes and an overcoat. And something—wasn't there something else? Ferris finished his drink and opened the telephone directory.

80   His decision to call his ex-wife was impulsive. The number was under Bailey, the husband's name, and he called before he had much time for self-debate. He and Elizabeth had exchanged cards at Christmastime, and Ferris had sent a carving set when he received the announcement of her wedding.
85   There was no reason *not* to call. But as he waited, listening to the ring at the other end, misgiving fretted him.

    Elizabeth answered; her familiar voice was a fresh shock to him. Twice he had to repeat his name, but when he was identified, she sounded glad. He explained he was only in town
90 for that day. They had a theater engagement, she said—but she wondered if he would come by for an early dinner. Ferris said he would be delighted.

    As he went from one engagement to another, he was still bothered at odd moments by the feeling that something neces-
95 sary was forgotten. Ferris bathed and changed in the late afternoon, often thinking about Jeannine: he would be with her the following night. "Jeannine," he would say, "I happened to run into my ex-wife when I was in New York. Had dinner with her. And her husband, of course. It was strange seeing her after all
100 these years."

    Elizabeth lived in the East Fifties, and as Ferris taxied uptown he glimpsed at intersections the lingering sunset, but by the time he reached his destination it was already autumn dark. The place was a building with a marquee and a doorman,
105 and the apartment was on the seventh floor.

    "Come in, Mr. Ferris."

    Braced for Elizabeth or even the unimagined husband, Ferris was astonished by the freckled red-haired child; he had known of the children, but his mind had failed somehow to
110 acknowledge them. Surprise made him step back awkwardly.

    "This is our apartment," the child said politely. "Aren't you Mr. Ferris? I'm Billy. Come in."

    In the living room beyond the hall, the husband provided another surprise; he too had not been acknowledged emotion-
115 ally. Bailey was a lumbering red-haired man with a deliberate manner. He rose and extended a welcoming hand.

"I'm Bill Bailey. Glad to see you. Elizabeth will be in, in a minute. She's finishing dressing."

The last words struck a gliding series of vibrations, memories of the other years. Fair Elizabeth, rosy and naked before her bath. Half-dressed before the mirror of her dressing table, brushing her fine, chestnut hair. Sweet, casual intimacy, the soft-fleshed loveliness indisputably possessed. Ferris shrank from the unbidden memories and compelled himself to meet Bill Bailey's gaze.

"Billy, would you please bring that tray of drinks from the kitchen table?"

The child obeyed promptly, and when he was gone Ferris remarked conversationally, "Fine boy you have there."

"We think so."

Flat silence until the child returned with a tray of glasses and a cocktail shaker of Martinis. With the priming drinks they pumped up conversation: Russia, they spoke of, and the New York rainmaking, and the apartment situation in Manhattan and Paris.

"Mr. Ferris is flying all the way across the ocean tomorrow," Bailey said to the little boy who was perched on the arm of his chair, quiet and well behaved. "I bet you would like to be a stowaway in his suitcase."

Billy pushed back his limp bangs. "I want to fly in an airplane and be a newspaperman like Mr. Ferris." He added with sudden assurance, "That's what I would like to do when I am big."

Bailey said, "I thought you wanted to be a doctor."

"I do!" said Billy. "I would like to be both. I want to be a atom-bomb scientist too."

Elizabeth came in carrying in her arms a baby girl.

"Oh, John!" she said. She settled the baby in the father's lap. "It's grand to see you. I'm awfully glad you could come."

The little girl sat demurely on Bailey's knees. She wore a pale pink crêpe de Chine frock, smocked around the yoke with rose, and a matching silk hair ribbon tying back her pale soft curls. Her skin was summer tanned and her brown eyes flecked with gold and laughing. When she reached up and fingered her father's horn-rimmed glasses, he took them off and let her look through them a moment. "How's my old Candy?"

Elizabeth was very beautiful, more beautiful perhaps than he had ever realized. Her straight clean hair was shining. Her face was softer, glowing and serene. It was a madonna loveli-
160 ness, dependent on the family ambiance.

"You've hardly changed at all," Elizabeth said, "but it has been a long time."

"Eight years." His hand touched his thinning hair self-consciously while further amenities were exchanged.

165 Ferris felt himself suddenly a spectator—an interloper among these Baileys. Why had he come? He suffered. His own life seemed so solitary, a fragile column supporting nothing amidst the wreckage of the years. He felt he could not bear much longer to stay in the family room.

170 He glanced at his watch. "You're going to the theater?"

"It's a shame," Elizabeth said, "but we've had this engagement for more than a month. But surely, John, you'll be staying here one of these days before long. You're not going to be an expatriate, are you?"

175 "Expatriate," Ferris repeated. "I don't much like the word."

"What's a better word?" she asked.

He thought for a moment. "Sojourner might do."

Ferris glanced again at his watch, and again Elizabeth apologized. "If only we had known ahead of time—"

180 "I just had this day in town. I came home unexpectedly. You see, Papa died last week."

"Papa Ferris is dead?"

"Yes, at Johns Hopkins. He had been sick there nearly a year. The funeral was down home in Georgia."

185 "Oh, I'm so sorry, John. Papa Ferris was always one of my favorite people."

The little boy moved from behind the chair so that he could look into his mother's face. He asked, "Who is dead?"

Ferris was oblivious to apprehension; he was thinking of
190 his father's death. He saw again the outstretched body on the quilted silk within the coffin. The corpse flesh was bizarrely rouged and the familiar hands lay massive and joined above a spread of funeral roses. The memory closed and Ferris awakened to Elizabeth's calm voice.

195 "Mr. Ferris' father, Billy. A really grand person. Somebody you didn't know."

"But why did you call him *Papa* Ferris?"

Bailey and Elizabeth exchanged a trapped look. It was Bailey who answered the questioning child. "A long time ago," he said, "your mother and Mr. Ferris were once married. Before you were born—a long time ago."

"Mr. Ferris?"

The little boy stared at Ferris, amazed and unbelieving. And Ferris' eyes, as he returned the gaze, were somehow unbelieving too. Was it indeed true that at one time he had called this stranger, Elizabeth, Little Butterduck during nights of love, that they had lived together, shared perhaps a thousand days and nights and—finally—endured in the misery of sudden solitude the fiber by fiber (jealousy, alcohol and money quarrels) destruction of the fabric of married love.

Bailey said to the children, "It's somebody's suppertime. Come on now."

"But Daddy! Mama and Mr. Ferris—I—"

Billy's everlasting eyes—perplexed and with a glimmer of hostility—reminded Ferris of the gaze of another child. It was the young son of Jeannine—a boy of seven with a shadowed little face and nobby knees whom Ferris avoided and usually forgot.

"Quick march!" Bailey gently turned Billy toward the door. "Say good night now, son."

"Good night, Mr. Ferris." He added resentfully, "I thought I was staying up for the cake."

"You can come in afterward for the cake," Elizabeth said. "Run along now with Daddy for your supper."

Ferris and Elizabeth were alone. The weight of the situation descended on those first moments of silence. Ferris asked permission to pour himself another drink and Elizabeth set the cocktail shaker on the table at his side. He looked at the grand piano and noticed the music on the rack.

"Do you still play as beautifully as you used to?"

"I still enjoy it."

"Please play, Elizabeth."

Elizabeth arose immediately. Her readiness to perform when asked had always been one of her amiabilities; she never hung back, apologized. Now as she approached the piano there was the added readiness of relief.

She began with a Bach prelude and fugue. The prelude was as gaily iridescent as a prism in a morning room. The first voice

of the fugue, an announcement pure and solitary, was repeated
240 intermingling with a second voice, and again repeated within
an elaborated frame, the multiple music, horizontal and serene,
flowed with unhurried majesty. The principal melody was
woven with two other voices, embellished with countless inge-
nuities—now dominant, again submerged, it had the sublimity
245 of a single thing that does not fear surrender to the whole.
Toward the end, the density of the material gathered for the last
enriched insistence on the dominant first motif and with a
chorded final statement the fugue ended. Ferris rested his head
on the chair back and closed his eyes. In the following silence a
250 clear, high voice came from the room down the hall.

"Daddy, how *could* Mama and Mr. Ferris—" A door was
closed.

The piano began again—what was this music? Unplaced,
familiar, the limpid melody had lain a long while dormant in
255 his heart. Now it spoke to him of another time, another
place—it was the music Elizabeth used to play. The delicate air
summoned a wilderness of memory. Ferris was lost in the riot
of past longings, conflicts, ambivalent desires. Strange that the
music, catalyst for this tumultuous anarchy, was so serene and
260 clear. The singing melody was broken off by the appearance of
the maid.

"Miz Bailey, dinner is out on the table now."

Even after Ferris was seated at the table between his host
and hostess, the unfinished music still overcast his mood. He
265 was a little drunk.

"*L'improvisation de la vie humaine,*" he said. "There's
nothing that makes you so aware of the improvisation of human
existence as a song unfinished. Or an old address book."

"Address book?" repeated Bailey. Then he stopped, non-
270 committal and polite.

"You're still the same old boy, Johnny," Elizabeth said with
a trace of the old tenderness.

It was a Southern dinner that evening, and the dishes were
his old favorites. They had fried chicken and corn pudding and
275 rich, glazed candied sweet potatoes. During the meal Elizabeth
kept alive a conversation when the silences were overlong.
And it came about that Ferris was led to speak of Jeannine.

"I first knew Jeannine last autumn—about this time of the
year—in Italy. She's a singer and she had an engagement in
280 Rome. I expect we will be married soon."

The words seemed so true, inevitable, that Ferris did not at first acknowledge to himself the lie. He and Jeannine had never in that year spoken of marriage. And indeed, she was still married—to a White Russian money-changer in Paris from whom she had been separated for five years. But it was too late to correct the lie. Already Elizabeth was saying: "This really makes me glad to know. Congratulations, Johnny."

He tried to make amends with truth. "The Roman autumn is so beautiful. Balmy and blossoming." He added, "Jeannine has a little boy of seven. A curious trilingual little fellow. We go to the Tuileries sometimes."

A lie again. He had taken the boy once to the gardens. The sallow foreign child in shorts that bared his spindly legs had sailed his boat in the concrete pond and ridden the pony. The child had wanted to go in to the puppet show. But there was not time, for Ferris had an engagement at the Scribe Hotel. He had promised they would go to the guignol another afternoon. Only once had he taken Valentin to the Tuileries.

There was a stir. The maid brought in a white-frosted cake with pink candles. The children entered in their night clothes. Ferris still did not understand.

"Happy birthday, John," Elizabeth said. "Blow out the candles."

Ferris recognized his birthday date. The candles blew out lingeringly and there was the smell of burning wax. Ferris was thirty-eight years old. The veins in his temples darkened and pulsed visibly.

"It's time you started for the theater."

Ferris thanked Elizabeth for the birthday dinner and said the appropriate good-byes. The whole family saw him to the door.

A high, thin moon shone above the jagged, dark skyscrapers. The streets were windy, cold. Ferris hurried to Third Avenue and hailed a cab. He gazed at the nocturnal city with the deliberate attentiveness of departure and perhaps farewell. He was alone. He longed for flighttime and the coming journey.

The next day he looked down on the city from the air, burnished in sunlight, toylike, precise. Then America was left behind and there was only the Atlantic and the distant European shore. The ocean was milky pale and placid beneath the clouds. Ferris dozed most of the day. Toward dark he was thinking of Elizabeth and the visit of the previous evening. He

thought of Elizabeth among her family with longing, gentle envy and inexplicable regret. He sought the melody, the unfin-
325 ished air, that had so moved him. The cadence, some unrelated tones, were all that remained; the melody itself evaded him. He found instead the first voice of the fugue that Elizabeth had played—it came to him, inverted mockingly and in a minor key. Suspended above the ocean the anxieties of transience
330 and solitude no longer troubled him and he thought of his father's death with equanimity. During the dinner hour the plane reached the shore of France.

At midnight Ferris was in a taxi crossing Paris. It was a clouded night and mist wreathed the lights of the Place de la
335 Concorde. The midnight bistros gleamed on the wet pave-ments. As always after a transocean flight the change of conti-nents was too sudden. New York at morning, this midnight Paris. Ferris glimpsed the disorder of his life: the succession of cities, of transitory loves; and time, the sinister glissando of
340 the years, time always.

"*Vite! Vite!*" he called in terror. "*Dépêchez-vous.*"

Valentin opened the door to him. The little boy wore paja-mas and an outgrown red robe. His gray eyes were shadowed and, as Ferris passed into the flat, they flickered momentarily.
345 "*J'attends Maman.*"

Jeannine was singing in a night club. She would not be home before another hour. Valentin returned to a drawing, squatting with his crayons over the paper on the floor. Ferris looked down at the drawing—it was a banjo player with notes
350 and wavy lines inside a comic-strip balloon.

"We will go again to the Tuileries."

The child looked up and Ferris drew him closer to his knees. The melody, the unfinished music that Elizabeth had played, came to him suddenly. Unsought, the load of memory
355 jettisoned—this time bringing only recognition and sudden joy.

"Monsieur Jean," the child said, "did you see him?"

Confused, Ferris thought only of another child—the freck-led, family-loved boy. "See who, Valentin?"

"Your dead papa in Georgia." The child added, "Was he
360 okay?"

Ferris spoke with rapid urgency: "We will go often to the Tuileries. Ride the pony and we will go into the guignol. We will see the puppet show and never be in a hurry any more."

"Monsieur Jean," Valentine said. "The guignol is now closed."
365 Again, the terror the acknowledgment of wasted years and
death. Valentin, responsive and confident, still nestled in his
arms. His cheek touched the soft cheek and felt the brush of
the delicate eyelashes. With inner desperation, he pressed the
child close—as though an emotion as protean as his love could
370 dominate the pulse of time.

[1950]

Understanding the Story

1. What does the first paragraph tell us about John Ferris's life? For example, where does he travel in "the twilight border between waking and sleeping" (line 1)? How do you think these dreams reflect his actual life?

2. Looking at his address book (lines 29–41) makes Ferris aware of the passage of time.

   a. How have his friends' lives changed since they were young? How has his life changed?

   b. What pain in Ferris's life has been soothed by "the anodyne of time" (line 65)? In the course of the story, how does he use liquor as a more temporary anodyne?

3. Three times during the day, Ferris has an uncomfortable feeling: "something unpleasant was awaiting him" (line 9), "something—wasn't there something else" (line 78), "something necessary was forgotten" (lines 94–95). What does the "something" turn out to be? In what sense is it "unpleasant" for him? In what sense is it "necessary"?

4. Although Ferris is excited by seeing Elizabeth again, he finds himself "lagging unaccountably" (line 53) as he is about to overtake her on the street. After having a drink, he makes an "impulsive" (line 80) decision to call her but then worries as the phone rings. What do you think explains this ambivalence—this pull in opposite directions—about seeing her?

5. Ferris is "astonished" (line 108) when Billy opens the door to greet him.

   a. What sort of boy is Billy? Why is Ferris so surprised to meet him?

   b. What would explain Billy's reaction—"[he] stared at Ferris, amazed and unbelieving" (line 203)— when he learns that Ferris was once married to his mother?

   c. Does Billy's reaction, as well as the way his parents handle the situation, seem realistic? Why or why not?

6. Seated in the Baileys' living room, Ferris sees himself as "a spectator," "an interloper," and "a fragile column supporting nothing amidst the wreckage of the years" (lines 165–68). In what way is each of these three descriptions appropriate?

7. At dinner, what is the first "lie" (line 282) that Ferris tells? What is the second? What leads him to tell these lies?

8. Ferris says (lines 266–68): "There's nothing that makes you so aware of the improvisation of human existence as a song unfinished. Or an old address book." What previous incidents in the story is he referring to? What do you think he means by his observation?

9. By the time Ferris reaches Paris, his anxiety about time passing has turned to "terror" (line 341). How are Billy and Valentin related to that change in feeling? What do the boys have in common? How are their lives different? (Consider, for example, the differences in their appearance.)

10. How does the title of the story fit John Ferris? In what ways is he a "sojourner"? What does it mean to call his love "protean" (line 369)?

Developing a Way with Words

1. Some words—such as *clear*—are often associated with pleasant ideas; that is, they have a positive connotation.

The words that mean the opposite are often associated with unpleasant ideas; that is, they have a negative connotation. Arrange the following words from the story in four positive/negative pairs. In the story, who is associated with the positive words? Who is associated with the negative ones?

amiable, clear, clouded, hostile, quiet, serene, shaken, tumultuous

2. The metaphors (implied comparisons) in the following sentences are printed in dark type. Discuss first the literal and then the figurative meaning of each metaphor.

   a. . . . but the years had somehow **unraveled** this filial devotion . . . (lines 24–25)

   b. With the **priming** drinks they **pumped up** conversation. (lines 132–33)

   c. The melody, the unfinished music that Elizabeth had played, came to him suddenly. Unsought, the load of memory **jettisoned**—this time bringing only recognition and sudden joy. (lines 353–55)

Making Connections

1. What sort of man is Ferris? What does he value? What things that he cared about has he lost? Why has he lost them?

2. Do you think it is likely that Ferris will marry Jeannine and settle down to a happy life with her and Valentin? Why or why not?

3. What do Jeannine and Valentin have in common with Elizabeth and Billy? In what ways could the lives of Billy and Valentin be said to mirror the lives of Elizabeth and Ferris?

   (One or the other of these questions could be the basis for a short paper.)

4. The story takes place within a period of forty-eight hours. At what time of day does each of Ferris's discoveries

take place? What time of year is it? How are the times of day and the season appropriate to the time Ferris has reached in his life?

5. Think about the people listed in Ferris's address book, Ferris himself, Elizabeth and Bill Bailey, and Jeannine. Which of them would you describe as successful in their lives? Why? If you could exchange places with any one of them, who would you choose to be? Why?

6. Ferris prefers "sojourner" to "expatriate." Why doesn't he like "expatriate"? What is the difference in connotation between the two words?

   a. Have you ever felt like a "sojourner," or an "expatriate," or both? What was the situation?

   b. Do you think it is possible to really feel at home in a second culture? Does living in a foreign country for an extended period make it impossible, in your opinion, to fit in again in one's home country? Why or why not?

   c. From what we know about the young man and woman in Ernest Hemingway's "Hills Like White Elephants," which term would best fit them? Why?

7. Many people feel that the death of a parent makes them understand for the first time that they, too, will die one day. Has one or both of your parents died? If so, did your experience at the time have anything in common with John Ferris's experience of his father's death? How is Ferris's experience like and unlike that of Jean, the narrator of Judy Troy's "Secrets"?

8. John Ferris and the Baileys in this story and Ted and Linda Turner in "The Orphaned Swimming Pool" by John Updike are members of the same social class. How are the lives of these two sets of characters similar? How are they different?

English as a Second Language

"'And Mama, you are going for an award for your English, for all you've learned, so please speak English!'"

English as a
Second Language

Lucy Honig
(born 1948)

Lucy Honig is a writer who has also taught English as a Second Language (ESL) in a number of adult education and intensive English-language programs in the New York City area. Her interests in teaching ESL and in writing fiction have emerged, she says, "from the same discomfort with 'mainstream' American culture—a need to get out of it, understand it, be with people who aren't in it either." Both interests are reflected in "English as a Second Language," which was honored by inclusion in *Prize Stories 1992: The O. Henry Awards.* "The story," Honig reports, "grew out of one of my first part-time teaching jobs, in a free adult education program. My students had come from all over the third world. In New York, they were struggling to live, struggling to be understood, and grasping for insider tips on how to fit in America."

Maria, the story's main character, is a middle-aged immigrant from Central America who lives in New York City and is enrolled in an ESL class at a community college. During a moment of relaxation at work, Maria's thoughts wander from the immediate present to other parts of her life. Then and at other times during the story, she suddenly relives the traumatic events of her last day at home in Guatemala, a country whose long and brutal civil strife reflects social, religious, and political differences within the country and the region. And at the end of a painful day, Maria finds herself remembering a classmate's description of tragic events that took place in the People's Republic of China during the social upheaval of the Cultural Revolution (1966–76).

The story moves back and forth in time: from New York in the present to Guatemala in the past. It also moves among several different locations in New York City: the Plaza Hotel on the southern edge of Central Park in Manhattan, Maria's apartment in the Bronx, and the auditorium of a community college near City Hall, an hour or more by subway from Maria's home.

Like many authors, Honig has used white space between paragraphs to signal changes of time and location. For additional emphasis, she has placed three asterisks (stars) after Maria's first memory of her last day at home in Guatemala. What do you suppose happened on that day? As you will see, the past and present become merged toward the end of the story. What do you suppose might cause that to happen? You may find that you recognize some of the students in Maria's ESL class. You may even recognize yourself.

Uncommon Words or Meanings

a vanity ("fluffy towels on the bathroom *vanity*")—a low shelf or table with a mirror above it.

a game show ("The big mouth *game show* host")—a television program in which contestants compete in a game to win prizes.

Saginaw ("a boyfriend back in *Saginaw*")—a town in Michigan.

a hookup ("No *hookups* for a washer")—a connection to supply water or electricity.

a spread ("carefully smoothed out the quilted *spread*")—a bedspread, the covering put over a bed during the day.

San _____ ("at the market in *San _____*")—a literary device suggesting that the author is thinking of a real town but is concealing its name.

the IRT ("the downtown *IRT*")—Interborough Rapid Transit, one of New York's three subway companies; the train is going south ("downtown") from the Bronx to Manhattan.

family planning ("advertisements for *family planning* and TWA")—birth control.

TWA ("advertisements for family planning and *TWA*")—Trans World Airlines.

to beam ("Maria *beamed* out at her")—to smile happily.

a G.E.D. ("pursuing her *G.E.D.* in Spanish")—General Equivalency Diploma, the equivalent of a high school diploma, earned by taking courses and passing examinations.

the 1986 Immigration Act ("amnesty under the *1986 Immigration Act*")—a U.S. law allowing any illegal immigrant who had entered the country before January 1, 1982 to apply for citizenship.

d'ya ("What *d'ya* think, the Republicans put her here . . . ?")—"do you."

the Republicans ("What d'ya think, *the Republicans* put her here . . . ?")—voters in one of the two major U.S. political parties; the vast majority of registered voters in New York City are Democrats.

the Board of Estimate ("or maybe the *Board of Estimate*")—at the time of the story, a small group, including the mayor, responsible for the New York City budget.

stout ("her own *stout* form")—tending to fatness.

enrapt ("people in the audience, looking ahead, *enrapt*")—paying complete attention.

Epsom salts ("soaking her feet in *Epsom salts*")—a white powder added to water to relieve pain.

Johnny ("The man called *Johnny* was on the screen, talking.")—Johnny Carson, for many years the highly popular host of a late-night television show.

a sweatshop ("sewed coats in a *sweatshop* all day")—a place where workers are employed at low wages for long hours under bad conditions.

the Staten Island Ferry ("took the subway to the *Staten Island Ferry*")—a boat providing regular public transportation between two boroughs of New York City in a thirty–minute crossing.

a provocation ("no reason, no *provocation*")—something that stirs one to action.

to furrow ("*furrowed* her forehead")—to wrinkle, make grooves in.

Inside Room 824, Maria parked the vacuum cleaner, fastened all the locks and the safety chain and kicked off her shoes. Carefully she lay a stack of fluffy towels on the bathroom vanity. She turned the air conditioning up high and the lights down low. Then she hoisted up the skirt of her uniform and settled all the way back on the king-sized bed with her legs straight out in front of her. Her feet and ankles were swollen. She wriggled her toes. She threw her arms out in each direction and still her hands did not come near the edges of the bed. From here she could see, out the picture window, the puffs of green treetops in Central Park, the tiny people circling along the paths below. She tore open a small foil bag of cocktail peanuts and ate them very slowly, turning each one over separately with her tongue until the salt dissolved. She snapped on the TV with the remote control and flipped channels.

The big mouth game show host was kissing and hugging a woman playing on the left-hand team. Her husband and children were right there with her, and *still* he encircled her with his arms. Then he sidled up to the daughter, a girl younger than her own Guiliette, and *hugged* her and kept *holding* her, asking questions. None of his business, if this girl had a boyfriend back in Saginaw!

"Mama, you just don't understand." That's what Jorge always said when she watched TV at home. He and his teenaged friends would sit around in their torn bluejeans dropping potato chips between the cushions of her couch and laughing, writhing with laughter while she sat like a stone.

Now the team on the right were hugging each other, squealing, jumping up and down. They'd just won a whole new kitchen—refrigerator, dishwasher, clothes washer, microwave, *everything!* Maria could win a whole new kitchen too, someday. You just spun a wheel, picked some words. She could do that.

She saw herself on TV with Carmen and Guiliette and Jorge. Her handsome children were so quick to press the buzzers the other team never had a chance to answer first. And they got every single answer right. Her children shrieked and clapped and jumped up and down each time the board lit up.

They kissed and hugged that man whenever they won a prize. That man put his hands on her beautiful young daughters. That man pinched and kissed *her*, an old woman, in front of the whole world! Imagine seeing *this* back home! Maria frowned, chewing on the foil wrapper. There was nobody left at home in Guatemala, nobody to care if a strange man squeezed her wrinkled flesh on the TV.

"Forget it, Mama. They don't let poor people on these programs," Jorge said one day.

"But poor people need the money, they can win it here!"

Jorge sighed impatiently. "They don't give it away because you *need* it!"

It was true, she had never seen a woman with her kids say on a show: My husband's dead. Jorge knew. They made sure before they invited you that you were the right kind of people and that you said the right things. Where would she put a new kitchen in her cramped apartment anyway? No hookups for a washer, no space for a two-door refrigerator.

She slid sideways off the bed, carefully smoothed out the quilted spread, and squeezed her feet into her shoes. Back out in the hall she counted the bath towels in her cart to see if there were enough for the next wing. Then she wheeled the cart down the corridor, silent on the deep blue rug.

Maria pulled the new pink dress on over her head, eased her arms into the sleeves, then let the skirt slide into place. In the mirror she saw a small dark protrusion from a large pink flower. She struggled to zip up in back, then she fixed the neck, attaching the white collar she had crocheted. She pinned the rhinestone brooch on next. Shaking the pantyhose out of the package, she remembered the phrase: the cow before the horse, wasn't that it? She should have put these on first. Well, so what. She rolled down the left leg of the nylons, stuck her big toe in, and drew the sheer fabric around her foot, unrolling it up past her knee. Then she did the right foot, careful not to catch the hose on the small flap of scar.

The right foot bled badly when she ran over the broken glass, over what had been the only window of the house. It had shattered from gunshots across the dirt yard. The chickens dashed around frantically, squawking, trying to fly, spraying

brown feathers into the air. When she had seen Pedro's head turn to blood and the two oldest boys dragged away, she swallowed every word, every cry, and ran with the two girls. The
80 fragments of glass stayed in her foot for all the days of hiding. They ran and ran and ran and somehow Jorge caught up and they were found by their own side and smuggled out. And still she was silent, until the nurse at the border went after the glass and drained the mess inside her foot. Then she had
85 sobbed and screamed, "Aaiiee!"

*   *   *

"Mama, stop thinking and get ready," said Carmen.

"It is too short, your skirt," Maria said in Spanish. "What will they say?"

Carmen laughed. "It's what they all wear, except for you
90 old ladies."

"Not to work! Not to school!"

"Yes, to work, to school! And Mama, you are going for an award for your English, for all you've learned, so please speak English!"

95 Maria squeezed into the pink high heels and held each foot out, one by one, so she could admire the beautiful slim arch of her own instep, like the feet of the American ladies on Fifth Avenue. Carmen laughed when she saw her mother take the first faltering steps, and Maria laughed too. How much she had
100 already practiced in secret, and still it was so hard! She teetered on them back and forth from the kitchen to the bedroom, trying to feel steady, until Carmen finally sighed and said, "Mama, quick now or you'll be late!"

She didn't know if it was a good omen or a bad one, the
105 two Indian women on the subway. They could have been sitting on the dusty ground at the market in San _____, selling corn or clay pots, with the bright-colored striped shawls and full skirts, the black hair pulled into two braids down each back, the deeply furrowed square faces set in those impassive
110 expressions, seeing everything, seeing nothing. They were exactly as they must have been back home, but she was seeing them *here*, on the downtown IRT from the Bronx, surrounded by businessmen in suits, kids with big radio boxes, girls in skin-tight jeans and dark purple lipstick. Above them, adver-
115 tisements for family planning and TWA. They were like stone-

age men sitting on the train in loincloths made from animal skins, so out of place, out of time. Yet timeless. Maria thought, they are timeless guardian spirits, here to accompany me to my honors. Did anyone else see them? As strange as they were, nobody looked. Maria's heart pounded faster. The boys with the radios were standing right over them and never saw them. They were invisible to everyone but her: Maria was utterly convinced of it. The spirit world had come back to life, here on the number 4 train! It was a miracle!

"Mama, look, you see the grandmothers?" said Carmen.

"Of course I see them" Maria replied trying to hide the disappointment in her voice. So Carmen saw them too. They were not invisible. Carmen rolled her eyes and smirked derisively as she nodded in their direction, but before she could put her derision into words, Maria became stern. "Have respect," she said. "They are the same as your father's people." Carmen's face sobered at once.

She panicked when they got to the big school by the river. "Like the United Nations," she said, seeing so much glass and brick, an endless esplanade of concrete.

"It's only a college, Mama. People learn English here, too. And more, like nursing, electronics. This is where Anna's brother came for computers."

"Las Naciones Unidas," Maria repeated, and when the guard stopped them to ask where they were going, she answered in Spanish: to the literacy awards ceremony.

"*English*, Mama!" whispered Carmen.

But the guard also spoke in Spanish: take the escalator to the third floor.

"See, he knows," Maria retorted.

"That's not the point," murmured Carmen, taking her mother by the hand.

Every inch of the enormous room was packed with people. She clung to Carmen and stood by the door paralyzed until Cheryl, her teacher, pushed her way to them and greeted Maria with a kiss. Then she led Maria back through the press of people to the small group of award winners from other programs. Maria smiled shakily and nodded hello.

"They're all here now!" Cheryl called out. A photographer
rushed over and began to move the students closer together
for a picture.

"Hey Bernie, wait for the Mayor!" someone shouted to him.
He spun around, called out some words Maria did not understand, and without even turning back to them, he disappeared.
But they stayed there, huddled close, not knowing if they
could move. The Chinese man kept smiling, the tall black man
stayed slightly crouched, the Vietnamese woman squinted,
confused, her glasses still hidden in her fist. Maria saw all the
cameras along the sides of the crowd, and the lights, and the
people from television with video machines, and more lights.
Her stomach began to jump up and down. Would she be on
television, in the newspapers? Still smiling, holding his pose,
the Chinese man next to her asked, "Are you nervous?"

"Oh yes," she said. She tried to remember the expression
Cheryl had taught them. "I have worms in my stomach," she said.

He was a much bigger man than she had imagined from
seeing him on TV. His face was bright red as they ushered him
into the room and quickly through the crowd, just as it was his
turn to take the podium. He said hello to the other speakers
and called them by their first names. The crowd drew closer to
the little stage, the people standing farthest in the back pushed
in. Maria tried hard to listen to the Mayor's words. "Great occasion . . . pride of our city . . . ever since I created the program
. . . people who have worked so hard . . . overcoming hardship
. . . come so far." Was that them? Was he talking about them
already? Why were the people out there all starting to laugh?
She strained to understand, but still caught only fragments of
his words. "My mother used to say . . . and I said, Look, Mama
. . ." He was talking about *his* mother now; he called her
Mama, just like Maria's kids called *her*. But everyone laughed
so hard. At his mother? She forced herself to smile; up front,
near the podium, everyone could see her. She should seem to
pay attention and understand. Looking out into the crowd she
felt dizzy. She tried to find Carmen among all the pretty young
women with big eyes and dark hair. There she was! Carmen's
eyes met Maria's; Carmen waved. Maria beamed out at her. For
a moment she felt like she belonged there, in this crowd.

Everyone was smiling, everyone was so happy while the Mayor of New York stood at the podium telling jokes. How
195   happy Maria felt too!

"Maria Perez grew up in the countryside of Guatemala, the oldest daughter in a family of 19 children," read the Mayor as Maria stood quaking by his side. She noticed he made a slight wheezing noise when he breathed between words. She
200   saw the hairs in his nostrils, black and white and wiry. He paused. "Nineteen children!" he exclaimed, looking at the audience. A small gasp was passed along through the crowd. Then the Mayor looked back at the sheet of paper before him. "Maria never had a chance to learn to read and write, and she
205   was already the mother of five children of her own when she fled Guatemala in 1980 and made her way to New York for a new start."
        It was her own story, but Maria had a hard time following. She had to stand next to him while he read it, and her feet had
210   started to hurt, crammed into the new shoes. She shifted her weight from one foot to the other.
        "At the age of 45, while working as a chambermaid and sending her children through school, Maria herself started school for the first time. In night courses she learned to read
215   and write in her native Spanish. Later, as she was pursuing her G.E.D. in Spanish, she began studying English as a Second Language. This meant Maria was going to school five nights a week! Still she worked as many as 60 hours cleaning rooms at the Plaza Hotel.
220   "Maria's ESL teacher, Cheryl Sands, says—and I quote— 'Maria works harder than any student I have ever had. She is an inspiration to her classmates. Not only has she learned to read and write in her new language, but she initiated an oral history project in which she taped and transcribed interviews
225   with other students, who have told their stories from around the world.' Maria was also one of the first in New York to apply for amnesty under the 1986 Immigration Act. Meanwhile, she has passed her enthusiasm for education to her children: her son is now a junior in high school, her youngest daughter
230   attends the State University, and her oldest daughter, who we are proud to have with us today, is in her second year of law school on a scholarship."

Two older sons were dragged through the dirt, chickens squawking in mad confusion, feathers flying. She heard more
235 gunshots in the distance, screams, chickens squawking. She heard, she ran. Maria looked down at her bleeding feet. Wedged tightly into the pink high heels, they throbbed.

The Mayor turned toward her. "Maria, I think it's wonderful that you have taken the trouble to preserve the folklore of
240 students from so many countries." He paused. Was she supposed to say something? Her heart stopped beating. What was folklore? What was preserved? She smiled up at him, hoping that was all she needed to do.

"Maria, tell us now, if you can, what was one of the stories
245 you collected in your project?"

This was definitely a question, meant to be answered. Maria tried to smile again. She strained on tiptoes to reach the microphone, pinching her toes even more tightly in her shoes. "Okay," she said, setting off a high-pitched ringing from the
250 microphone.

The Mayor said, "Stand back," and tugged at her collar. She quickly stepped away from the microphone.

"Okay," she said again, and this time there was no shrill sound. "One of my stories, from Guatemala. You want to hear?"
255 The Mayor put his arm around her shoulder and squeezed hard. Her first impulse was to wriggle away, but he held tight. "Isn't she wonderful?" he asked the audience. There was a low ripple of applause. "Yes, we want to hear!"

She turned and looked up at his face. Perspiration was
260 shining on his forehead and she could see by the bright red bulge of his neck that his collar was too tight. "In my village in Guatemala," she began, "the mayor did not go along—get along—with the government so good."

"Hey, Maria," said the Mayor, "I know exactly how he felt!"
265 The people in the audience laughed. Maria waited until they were quiet again.

"One day our mayor met with the people in the village. Like you meet people here. A big crowd in the square."

"The people liked him, your mayor?"
270 "Oh, yes," said Maria. "Very much. He was very good. He tried for more roads, more doctors, new farms. He cared very much about his people."

The Mayor shook his head up and down. "Of course," he said, and again the audience laughed.

275 Maria said, "The next day after the meeting, the meeting in the square with all the people, soldiers come and shoot him dead."

For a second there was total silence. Maria realized she had not used the past tense and felt a deep, horrible stab of shame
280 for herself, shame for her teacher. She was a disgrace! But she did not have more than a second of this horror before the whole audience began to laugh. What was happening? They couldn't be laughing at her bad verbs? They couldn't be laughing at her dead mayor! They laughed louder and louder and suddenly
285 flashbulbs were going off around her, the TV cameras swung in close, too close, and the Mayor was grabbing her by the shoulders again, holding her tight, posing for one camera after another as the audience burst into wild applause. But she hadn't even finished ! Why were they laughing?

290 "What timing, huh?" said the Mayor over the uproar. "What d'ya think, the Republicans put her here, or maybe the Board of Estimate?" Everyone laughed even louder and he still clung to her and cameras still moved in close, lights kept going off in her face and she could see nothing but the sharp white poof!
295 of light over and over again. She looked for Carmen and Cheryl, but the white poof! poof! poof! blinded her. She closed her eyes and listened to the uproar, now beginning to subside, and in her mind's eye saw chickens trying to fly, chickens fluttering around the yard littered with broken glass.

300 He squeezed her shoulders again and leaned into the microphone. "There are ways to get rid of mayors, and ways to get rid of mayors, huh Maria?"

The surge of laughter rose once more, reached a crescendo, and then began to subside again. "But wait," said
305 the Mayor. The cameramen stepped back a bit, poising themselves for something new.

"I want know just one more thing, Maria," said the Mayor, turning to face her directly again. The crowd quieted. He waited a few seconds more, then asked his question. "It says
310 here 19 children. What was it like growing up in a house with 19 children? How many *bathrooms* did you have?"

Her stomach dropped and twisted as the mayor put his hand firmly on the back of her neck and pushed her toward the

microphone again. It was absolutely quiet now in the huge
315 room. Everyone was waiting for her to speak. She cleared her
throat and made the microphone do the shrill hum. Startled,
she jumped back. Then there was silence. She took a big, trem-
bling breath.

"We had no bathrooms there, Mister Mayor," she said.
320 "Only the outdoors."

The clapping started immediately, then the flashbulbs
burning up in her face. The Mayor turned to her, put a hand on
each of her shoulders, bent lower and kissed her! Kissed her
on the cheek!

325 "Isn't she terrific?" he asked the audience, his hand on the
back of her neck again, drawing her closer to him. The audience clapped louder, faster. "Isn't she just the greatest?"

She tried to smile and open her eyes, but the lights were
still going off—poof! poof—and the noise was deafening.

330 "Mama, look, your eyes were closed *there*, too," chided
Jorge, sitting on the floor in front of the television set.

Maria had watched the camera move from the announcer
at the studio desk to her own stout form in bright pink, standing by the Mayor.

335 "In my village in Guatemala," she heard herself say, and the
camera showed her wrinkled face close up, eyes open now but
looking nowhere. Then the mayor's face filled the screen, his
forehead glistening, and then suddenly all the people in the
audience, looking ahead, enrapt, took his place. Then there
340 was her wrinkled face again, talking without a smile ". . . soldiers come and shoot him dead." Maria winced, hearing the
wrong tense of her verbs. The camera shifted from her face to
the Mayor. In the brief moment of shamed silence after she'd
uttered those words, the Mayor drew his finger like a knife
345 across his throat. And the audience began to laugh.

"Turn it off!" she yelled to Jorge. "Off! This minute!"

Late that night she sat alone in the unlighted room, soaking
her feet in Epsom salts. The glow of the television threw shadows across the wall, but the sound was off. The man called
350 Johnny was on the screen, talking. The people in the audience
and the men in the band and the movie stars sitting on the
couch all had their mouths wide open in what she knew were

screams of laughter while Johnny wagged his tongue. Maria heard nothing except brakes squealing below on the street and
355 the lonely clanging of garbage cans in the alley.

She thought about her English class and remembered the pretty woman, Ling, who often fell asleep in the middle of a lesson. The other Chinese students all teased her. Everyone knew that she sewed coats in a sweatshop all day. After the
360 night class she took the subway to the Staten Island Ferry, and after the ferry crossing she had to take a bus home. Her parents were old and sick and she did all their cooking and cleaning late at night. She struggled to keep awake in class; it seemed to take all her energy simply to smile and
365 listen. She said very little and the teacher never forced her, but she fell further and further behind. They called her the Quiet One.

One day just before the course came to an end the Quiet One asked to speak. There was no reason, no provocation—
370 they'd been talking informally about their summer plans—but Ling spoke with a sudden urgency. Her English was very slow. Seeing what a terrible effort it was for her, the classmates all tried to help when she searched for words.

"In my China village there was a teacher," Ling began. "Man
375 teacher." She paused. "All children love him. He teach mathematic. He very—" She stopped and looked up toward the ceiling. Then she gestured with her fingers around her face.

"Handsome!" said Charlene, the oldest of the three Haitian sisters in the class.
380 Ling smiled broadly. "Handsome! Yes, he very handsome. Family very rich before. He have sister go to Hong Kong who have many, many money."

"*Much* money," said Maria.

"Much, much money," repeated Ling thoughtfully. "Teacher
385 live in big house."

"In China? Near you?"

"Yes. Big house with much old picture." She stopped and furrowed her forehead, as if to gather words inside of it.

"Art? Paint? Pictures like that?" asked Xavier.
390 Ling nodded eagerly. "Yes. In big house. Most big house in village."

"But big house, money, rich like that, bad in China," said Fu Wu. "Those year, Government bad to you. How they let him do?"

"In *my* country," said Carlos, "government bad to you if you got *small* house, *no* money."

"Me too," said Maria.

"Me too," said Charlene.

The Chinese students laughed.

Ling shrugged and shook her head. "Don't know. He have big house. Money gone, but keep big house. Then I am little girl." She held her hand low to the floor.

"I *was* a little girl," Charlene said gently.

"I *was*," said Ling. "Was, was." She giggled for a moment, then seemed to spend some time in thought. "We love him. All children love—all children did loved him. He giving tea in house. He was—was—so handsome!" She giggled. All the women in the class giggled. "He very nice. He learn music, he go . . . he went to school far away."

"America?"

Ling shook her head. "Oh no, no. You know, another . . . west."

"Europa!" exclaimed Maria proudly. "Espain!"

"No, no, another."

"France!" said Patricia, Charlene's sister. "He went to school in France?"

"Yes, France," said Ling. Then she stopped again, this time for a whole minute. The others waited patiently. No one said a word. Finally she continued. "But big boys in more old school not like him. He too handsome."

"Oooh!" sang out a chorus of women. "Too handsome!"

"The boys were jealous," said Carlos.

Ling seized the word. "Jealous! Jealous! They very jealous. He handsome, he study France, he very nice to children, he give tea and cake in big house, he show picture on wall." Her torrent of words came to an end and she began to think again, visibly, her brow furrowing. "Big school boys, they . . ." She stopped.

"Jealous!" sang out the others.

"Yes," she said, shaking her head "no." "But more. More bad. Hate. They hate him."

"That's bad," said Patricia.

"Yes, very bad." Ling paused, looking at the floor. "And they heat."

"Hate."

"No, they heat."

All the class looked puzzled. Heat? Heat? They turned to Cheryl.

The teacher spoke for the first time. "Hit? Ling, do you mean hit? They hit him?" Cheryl slapped the air with her hand.

Ling nodded, her face somehow serious and smiling at the same time. "Hit many time. And also so." She scooted her feet back and forth along the floor.

"Oooh," exclaimed Charlene, frowning. "They kicked him with the feet."

"Yes," said Ling. "They kicked him with the feet and hit him with the hands, many many time they hit, they kick."

"Where this happened?" asked Xavier.

"In the school. In classroom like . . ." She gestured to mean their room.

"In the school?" asked Xavier. "But other people were they there? They say stop, no?"

"No. Little children in room. They cry, they . . ." She covered her eyes with her hand, then uncovered them. "Big boys kick and hit. No one stop. No one help."

Everyone in class fell silent. Maria remembered: they could not look at one another then. The could not look at their teacher.

Ling continued. "They break him, very hurt much place." She stopped. They all fixed their stares on Ling, they could bear looking only at her. "Many place," she said. Her face had not changed, it was still half smiling. But now there were drops coming from her eyes, a single tear down each side of her nose. Maria would never forget it. Ling's face did not move or wrinkle or frown. He body was absolutely still. Her shoulders did not quake. Nothing in the shape or motion of her eyes or mouth changed. None of the things that Maria had always known happen when you cry happened when Ling shed tears. Just two drops rolled slowly down her two pale cheeks as she smiled.

"He very hurt. He *was* very hurt. He blood many place. Boys go away. Children cry. Teacher break and hurt. Later he in hospital. I go there visit him." She stopped, looking thoughtful. "I went there." One continuous line of wetness glistened down each cheek. "My mother, my father say don't go, but I see him. I say, 'You be better?' But he hurt. Doctors no did helped.

475 He alone. No doctor. No nurse. No medicine. No family." She
stopped. They all stared in silence for several moments.

Finally Carlos said, "Did he went home?"

Ling shook her head. "He go home but no walk." She
stopped. Maria could not help watching those single lines of
480 tears moving down the pale round face. "A year, more, no
walk. Then go."

"Go where?"

"End."

Again there was a deep silence. Ling looked down, away
485 from them, her head bent low.

"Oh, no," murmured Charlene. "He died."

Maria felt the catch in her throat, the sudden wetness of tears
on her own two cheeks, and when she looked up she saw that all
the other students, men and women both, were crying too.

490 Maria wiped her eyes. Suddenly all her limbs ached, her
bones felt stiff and old. She took her feet from the basin and
dried them with a towel. Then she turned off the television and
went to bed.

[1992]

Understanding the Story

1. In the opening section of the story (lines 1–60), the
   reader is left to infer—to discover by reasoning from
   clues—just who Maria is.

   a. Where is Maria as the story opens? What does she do
      for a living? Where is she from?

   b. How many children does she have? Where is her hus-
      band?

2. What, specifically, does Maria disapprove of in the way
   TV game show hosts behave? How does her reaction to
   television programs differ from her children's reaction
   to them?

3. As Maria is putting on her new dress, she suddenly thinks
   of a violent event in her past. What triggers the memory?

What new information does the memory provide about her background?

4. The cultural gap between Maria and her children, first shown in their comments on television game shows, is presented more dramatically when Maria sees two Latin American Indian women on the subway (lines 104–32).

   a. How does Maria see the women?

   b. How does her daughter see them?

   c. What would explain why Maria and her daughter interpret the same sight so differently?

5. Several kinds of irony, explained below, can be found in the awards ceremony.

   a. Two people have completely different expectations of a single event, without either being aware of what the other expects.

   What does the awards ceremony mean to Maria?

   What do you suppose it means to the mayor?

   How is the mayor's behavior similar to that of the TV game show host? That is, how does the game show foreshadow (give a hint about something coming later) the awards ceremony?

   b. The reader knows something important about a character in the story that another character doesn't know.

   The mayor's introduction (lines 196–232) provides some new information about Maria, but what important details of her life does the reader know that the mayor doesn't?

   c. Two people believe they're talking about the same thing when they aren't; the reader knows they have misunderstood each other, but they don't.

   The mayor refers to Maria's oral history project as "preserv[ing] folklore" (line 239). What does "folklore" suggest? That is, what kind of story is the mayor expecting to hear? How is that different from the story that Maria tells (lines 261–77)?

d. Something happens for a reason that almost everyone, including the reader, understands; one character, however, completely misunderstands the cause.

What does Maria think causes the "total silence" (line 278) at the end of her story? When the audience then begins to laugh, what does she think the reason must be?

The reader learns the reason for the laughter when, later that night, Maria and her family see her part of the ceremony on the eleven o'clock news (lines 335–45). Why was the audience laughing? Why does Maria still not understand the reason for the laughter?

6. Maria's story concludes with her memory (lines 368–489) of another student's story.

   a. Why hadn't Ling talked all semester? What might explain her "sudden urgency" (line 371) to tell her story at the end of the semester?

   b. In the course of the story, what facts does Ling tell about her mathematics teacher in China? For example, what subject had he studied in France? Why were the boys at the school in China jealous of him?

   c. Why do you think "all the other students, men and women both, were crying too" (lines 488–89) when Ling finished?

7. Maria has been able to remember horrifying incidents in her own life but to continue with what she has been doing. Why do you think she suddenly feels "stiff and old" (line 491) after concluding her memory of Ling's story?

Developing a Way with Words

1. For each of the following idioms, try to find the correct word to replace the one in dark type. What does each of the idioms mean?

a. putting the **cow** before the horse (lines 67–68)

Hint: What is a four-letter word beginning with *c* for something that a horse pulls?

b. having **worms** in her stomach (line 170)

Hint: Some kinds of "worms" turn into beautiful flying insects. What is the insect?

2. A metaphor explains one thing by describing it in terms of something else. Examine the metaphors, printed in dark type, in the following sentences.

a. In the mirror she saw **a small dark protrusion from a large pink flower.** (lines 63–64)

When Maria looked at herself in the mirror after putting on her new dress, what "large pink flower" did she see?

What was the "small dark protrusion" sticking out of the "flower"?

b. The chickens dashed around frantically, squawking, trying to fly, **spraying brown feathers in the air.** (lines 75–77)

Sending a liquid through an opening with small holes makes the liquid spray; what made the feathers spray?

Making Connections

1. Do you think Maria's cultural misunderstandings with her children and the mayor are realistic? Why or why not? What experiences, if any, have you had of the same sort?

2. Despite the family's many problems, both Maria and her children are leading successful lives. What do you think accounts for their success? How is Maria's family similar to and different from immigrant families that you know?

3. Have you had the experience of being honored at an awards ceremony? If so, what did your experience have in common with Maria's? How was it different? If you had been in Maria's place at the awards ceremony in the story, how do you think you would have reacted to the mayor's comments?

4. Do you suppose the author invented Maria's and Ling's "folklore" stories, or do you think they might be real ones that the author heard from her students? Why? Does it seem possible, or probable, that such stories will become part of the folklore of future generations?

5. How did the other students and the teacher help Ling to tell her story? Which ways seemed to work best? Would the story have been more effective if Ling had told it more fluently? Why or why not? In Maria and Ling's class, what are the students learning besides English grammar and vocabulary?

6. When you are in Ling's position of trying to explain a complicated situation or idea without having all the words you need, what strategies do you use? What kinds of help do you find most useful in a situation like that?

7. Have you or someone you know had an experience of terror? If so, would you be willing to talk or write about it?

The Bass, the River, and Sheila Mant

"There was a summer in my life when the only creature that seemed lovelier to me than a largemouth bass was Sheila Mant."

The Bass, the River, and Sheila Mant

W. D. Wetherell
(born 1948)

W. D. Wetherell is the author of seven books, including the novel *Chekov's Sister* (1990) and the essay collection *Upland Stream* (1992), which is subtitled "Notes on the Fishing Passion." He was born in Garden City, New York, not far from the setting of the title story in his collection *The Man Who Loved Levittown* (1985), which also includes "The Bass, the River, and Sheila Mant." Wetherell, who is a professor in the Master of Fine Arts program at Vermont College, lives with his family in rural New Hampshire. From his writing desk, a thousand yards to the west he can see the Connecticut River, which is the river of the bass and Sheila.

Sheila and the boy in the story, as well as their creator, Wetherell, are members of the baby-boom generation, the sons and daughters of the World War II veterans who returned home with money to spend and lost years to make up for. In the New York City area, those with professional skills bought homes in new communities like Garden City. Many blue-collar workers bought smaller, less expensive homes farther out on Long Island in Levittown, the prototypical planned community in the United States. The nearby Grumman Aircraft plant provided employment for many of those veterans, as it shifted to peacetime products such as aluminum canoes and lunar landers. The wives and children of the white-collar workers often spent the summer in a northern state, while the husbands remained at work in the hot, non-air-conditioned city. Sheila Mant was surely the daughter of such a middle-class family, rather than of wealthy parents, as today's readers might think, for it was normal for baby-boomers to expect to get everything.

While "The Bass, the River, and Sheila Mant" at first seems as undatable as any fishing story, it is carefully set in a specific time—the early 1960s. The clues are the aluminum canoe (which is shined up with a Brillo scouring pad), a transistor radio, and a Mitchell reel and Pfluger rod. This careful introduction of technological advances and brand names reaches its dramatic peak when a Corvette—the devastatingly sexy, quintessential sports car of the period—is used to deliver a stunning blow.

Uncommon Words or Meanings

a largemouth bass ("the only creature that seemed lovelier to me than a *largemouth bass*")—a North American freshwater fish whose mouth is so large that it can swallow a frog or even a duckling.

too (noisy) by half ("'*Too noisy by half*,' my mother quickly decided.")—(idiom) excessively (noisy).

all but ("at seventeen, *all but* out of reach")—nearly, almost.

a float ("a *float* my Uncle Sierbert had moored")—a floating platform attached to a dock.

Dartmouth ("the *Dartmouth* heavyweight crew")—one of the eight prestigious Ivy League colleges, for men only at the time of the story. Dartmouth is in Hanover, New Hampshire, several miles south of this story's setting.

a crew ("heavyweight *crew*")—a team of eight rowers and a coxswain, who directs them.

the [Australian] crawl ("the beauty of my flutter kick, the power of my *crawl*")—a swimming stroke.

to sear ("have been *seared* from my memory")—to cause to wither or dry up.

the brunt ("I took the full *brunt* of her long red hair")—the main force or impact.

Brillo ("rubbed every inch with *Brillo*")—a brand name for a pad of steel wool with soap in it.

chamois ("wiping it with *chamois*")—soft leather made from the skin of a deer, sheep, or goat.

a thwart ("propping up my father's transistor radio by the middle *thwart*")—a wood or metal brace extending from one side of a canoe to the other.

a rod and reel ("I mounted my Mitchell *reel* on my Pfluger spinning *rod*")—a fishing pole (**rod**) with an attached spool (**reel**) for letting out or winding up the line.

a cast ("in our driveway practicing *casts*")—the action of throwing a baited hook or lure (defined below) with a fishing rod.

drag ("to test the reel's *drag*")—the slippage of the reel, without which the line would break if a fish suddenly pulled hard.

a plug ("I tied on a big Rapala *plug*")—a wooden or plastic cylinder that often resembles a bait fish.

tense ("Parking's *tense* up there.")—difficult.

to pry ("I *pried* the canoe away from the dock")—to move using a lever-like action.

to stroke ("he *strokes* number four")—to hold a position on a crew team.

to write (something) off ("*written off* forty or so dollars as love's tribute")—(idiom) to admit and accept that (something) is a loss or failure.

a lure ("Fish will trail a *lure*")—a shiny metal spoon-like object that flashes to attract a fish.

an inhibition ("enough to overcome the bass's *inhibitions*")—an inner check or restraint that prevents an action based on impulse or desire.

a concussion ("landing with a *concussion* heavy enough to . . .")—a violent shaking or shock.

a fraternity ("These *fraternity* men.")—a social club for a group of male students.

UVM; Bennington ("I'm thinking more of *UVM* or *Bennington*")—the University of Vermont at Montpelier; Bennington College.

Ann-Margret ("I mean, *Ann-Margret*? Like hers, only shorter.")—an actress who was a movie starlet in the 1960s.

no sweat ("*No sweat,* or anything.")—(slang) easily done or handled; no problem.

a gape ("the *gape* of its mouth")—a broad opening.

a covered bridge ("beneath a *covered bridge*")—a wooden bridge with walls and a roof to protect it from snow, found in New England.

Jackie Kennedy ("I saw *Jackie Kennedy* in Boston")—Jacqueline Kennedy Onassis, at the time of the story, the First Lady of the United States and a trendsetter in fashion.

to whine ("'My legs are sore,' Sheila *whined.*")—to speak in a self-pitying, complaining tone.

a Corvette ("going home in Eric Caswell's *Corvette*")—a two-seater Chevrolet sports car, introduced in 1953, known for its powerful engine and sexy styling.

a spell ("the *spell* she cast over me")—magic used to control someone's thoughts or actions.

to haunt ("that lost bass *haunted* me all summer")—to return to the mind repeatedly.

The Bass, the River, and Sheila Mant

There was a summer in my life when the only creature that seem lovelier to me than a largemouth bass was Sheila Mant. I was fourteen. The Mants had rented the cottage next to ours on the river; with their parties, their frantic games of softball,
5 their constant comings and goings, they appeared to me denizens of a brilliant existence. "Too noisy by half," my mother quickly decided, but I would have given anything to be invited to one of their parties, and when my parents went to bed I would sneak through the woods to their hedge and stare
10 enchanted at the candlelit swirl of white dresses and bright, paisley skirts.

Sheila was the middle daughter—at seventeen, all but out of reach. She would spend her days sunbathing on a float my Uncle Sierbert had moored in their cove, and before July was
15 over I had learned all her moods. If she lay flat on the diving board with her hand trailing idly in the water, she was pensive, not to be disturbed. On her side, her head propped up by her arm, she was observant, considering those around her with a look that seemed queenly and severe. Sitting up, arms tucked
20 around her long, suntanned legs, she was approachable, but barely, and it was only in those glorious moments when she stretched herself prior to entering the water that her various suitors found the courage to come near.

These were many. The Dartmouth heavyweight crew
25 would scull by her house on their way upriver, and I think all eight of them must have been in love with her at various times during the summer; the coxswain would curse at them through his megaphone, but without effect—there was always a pause in their pace when they passed Sheila's float. I sup-
30 pose to these jaded twenty-year-olds she seemed the incarnation of innocence and youth, while to me she appeared unutterably suave, the epitome of sophistication. I was on the swim team at school, and to win her attention would do endless laps between my house and the Vermont shore, hoping
35 she would notice the beauty of my flutter kick, the power of my crawl. Finishing, I would boost myself up onto our dock and glance casually over toward her, but she was never watch-

ing, and the miraculous day she was, I immediately climbed
the diving board and did my best tuck and a half for her, and
40 continued diving until she had left and the sun went down and
my longing was like a madness and I couldn't stop.

It was late August by the time I got up the nerve to ask her
out. The tortured will-I's, won't-I's, the agonized indecision
over what to say, the false starts toward her house and embar-
45 rassed retreats—the details of these have been seared from my
memory, and the only part I remember clearly is emerging
from the woods toward dusk while they were playing softball
on their lawn, as bashful and frightened as a unicorn.

Sheila was stationed halfway between first and second,
50 well outside the infield. She didn't seem surprised to see me—
as a matter of fact, she didn't seem to see me at all.

"If you're playing second base, you should move closer," I
said.

She turned—I took the full brunt of her long red hair and
55 well-spaced freckles.

"I'm playing outfield," she said, "I don't like the responsibil-
ity of having a base."

"Yeah, I can understand that," I said, though I couldn't.
"There's a band in Dixford tomorrow night at nine. Want to
60 go?"

One of her brothers sent the ball sailing over the left-
fielder's head; she stood and watched it disappear toward the
river.

"You have a car?" she said, without looking up.
65 I played my master stroke. "We'll go by canoe."

I spent all of the following day polishing it. I turned it
upside down on our lawn and rubbed every inch with Brillo,
hosing off the dirt, wiping it with chamois until it gleamed as
bright as aluminum ever gleamed. About five, I slid it into the
70 water, arranging cushions near the bow to Sheila could lean on
them if she was in one of her pensive moods, propping up my
father's transistor radio by the middle thwart so we could have
music when we came back. Automatically, without thinking
about it, I mounted my Mitchell reel on my Pfluger spinning
75 rod and stuck it in the stern.

I say automatically, because I never went anywhere that
summer without a fishing rod. When I wasn't swimming laps to
impress Sheila, I was back in our driveway practicing casts, and

when I wasn't practicing casts, I was tying the line to Tosca, our
80   springer spaniel, to test the reel's drag, and when I wasn't doing
any of those things, I was fishing the river for bass.

Too nervous to sit at home, I got in the canoe early and
started paddling in a huge circle that would get me to Sheila's
dock around eight. As automatically as I brought along my rod,
85   I tied on a big Rapala plug, let it down into the water, let out
some line and immediately forgot all about it.

It was already dark by the time I glided up to the Mants'
dock. Even by day the river was quiet, most of the summer
people preferring Sunapee or one of the other nearby lakes,
90   and at night it was a solitude difficult to believe, a corridor of
hidden life that ran between banks like a tunnel. Even the stars
were part of it. They weren't as sharp anywhere else; they
seemed to have chosen the river as a guide on their slow wheel
toward morning, and in the course of the summer's fishing, I
95   had learned all their names.

I was there ten minutes before Sheila appeared. I heard the
slam of their screen door first, then saw her in the spotlight as
she came slowly down the path. As beautiful as she was on the
float, she was even lovelier now—her white dress went per-
100 fectly with her hair, and complimented her figure even more
than her swimsuit.

It was her face that bothered me. It had on its delightful
fullness a very dubious expression.

"Look," she said. "I can get Dad's car."
105 "It's faster this way," I lied. "Parking's tense up there. Hey,
it's safe. I won't tip it or anything."

She let herself down reluctantly into the bow. I was glad
she wasn't facing me. When her eyes were on me, I felt like diving in the river again from agony and joy.
110 I pried the canoe away from the dock and started paddling
upstream. There was an extra paddle in the bow, but Sheila
made no move to pick it up. She took her shoes off, and dan-
gled her feet over the side.

Ten minutes went by.
115 "What kind of band?" she said.
"It's sort of like folk music. You'll like it."
"Eric Caswell's going to be there. He strokes number four."
"No kidding?" I said. I had no idea who she meant.
"What's that sound?" she said pointing toward shore.

120   "Bass. That splashing sound?"

"Over there."

"Yeah, bass. They come into the shallows at night to chase frogs and moths and things. Big largemouths. *Micropetrus salmonides*," I added, showing off.

125   "I think fishing's dumb," she said, making a face. "I mean, it's boring and all. Definitely dumb."

Now I have spent a great deal of time in the years since wondering why Sheila Mant should come down so hard on fishing. Was her father a fisherman? Her antipathy toward fishing nothing more than normal filial rebellion? Had she tried it once? A messy encounter with worms? It doesn't matter. What does, is that at that fragile moment in time I would have given anything not to appear dumb in Sheila's severe and unforgiving eyes.

She hadn't seen my equipment yet. What I *should* have done, of course, was push the canoe in closer to shore and carefully slide the rod into some branches where I could pick it up again in the morning. Failing that, I could have surreptitiously dumped the whole outfit overboard, written off the forty or so dollars as love's tribute. What I actually *did* do was gently lean forward, and slowly, every so slowly, push the rod back through my legs toward the stern where it would be less conspicuous.

It must have been just exactly what the bass was waiting for. Fish will trail a lure sometimes, trying to make up their mind whether or not to attack, and the slight pause in the plug's speed caused by my adjustment was tantalizing enough to overcome the bass's inhibitions. My rod, safely out of sight at last, bent double. The line, tightly coiled, peeled off the spool with the shrill, tearing zip of a high-speed drill.

Four things occurred to me at once. One, that it was a bass. Two, that it was a big bass. Three, that it was the biggest bass I had ever hooked. Four, that Sheila Mant must not know.

"What was that?" she said, turning half around.

"Uh, what was what?"

"That buzzing noise."

155   "Bats."

She shuddered, quickly drew her feet back into the canoe. Every instinct I had told me to pick up the rod and strike back at the bass, but there was no need to—it was already solidly hooked. Downstream, an awesome distance downstream, it jumped clear of the water, landing with a concussion heavy enough to ripple the entire river. For a moment, I thought it was gone, but then the rod was bending again, the tip dancing into the water. Slowly, not making any motion that might alert Sheila, I reached down to tighten the drag.

165   While all this was going on, Sheila had begun talking and it was a few minutes before I was able to catch up with her train of thought.

"I went to a party there. These fraternity men. Katherine says I could get in there if I wanted. I'm thinking more of UVM 170   or Bennington. Somewhere I can ski."

The bass was slanting toward the rocks on the New Hampshire side by the ruins of Donaldson's boathouse. It had to be an old bass—a young one probably wouldn't have known the rocks were there. I brought the canoe back out into the middle 175   of the river, hoping to head it of.

"That's neat," I mumbled. "Skiing. Yeah, I can see that."

"Eric said I have the figure to model, but I thought I should get an education first. I mean, it might be a while before I get started and all. I was thinking of getting my hair styled, more 180   swept back? I mean, Ann-Margret? Like hers, only shorter."

She hesitated. "Are we going backwards?"

We were. I had managed to keep the bass in the middle of the river away from the rocks, but it had plenty of room there, and for the first time a chance to exert its full strength. I 185   quickly computed the weight necessary to draw a fully loaded canoe backwards—the thought of it made me feel faint.

"It's just the current," I said hoarsely. "No sweat or anything."

I dug in deeper with my paddle. Reassured, Sheila began 190   talking about something else, but all my attention was taken up now with the fish. I could feel its desperation as the water grew shallower. I could sense the extra strain on the line, the frantic way it cut back and forth in the water. I could visualize what it looked like—the gape of its mouth, the flared gills and 195   thick vertical tail. The bass couldn't have encountered many forces in its long life that it wasn't capable of handling, and the unrelenting tug at its mouth must have been a source of great puzzlement and mounting panic.

Me, I had problems of my own. To get to Dixford, I had to 200   paddle up a sluggish stream that came into the river beneath a covered bridge. There was a shallow sandbar at the mouth of this stream—weeds on one side, rocks on the other. Without doubt, this is where I would lose the fish.

"I have to be careful with my complexion. I tan, but in segments. I can't figure out if it's even worth it. I wouldn't even do it probably. I saw Jackie Kennedy in Boston and she wasn't tan at all."

Taking a deep breath, I paddled as hard as I could for the middle, deepest part of the bar. I could have threaded the eye of a needle with the canoe, but the pull on the stern threw me off and I overcompensated—the canoe veered left and scraped bottom. I pushed the paddle down and shoved. A moment of hesitation . . . a moment more. . . . The canoe shot clear into the deeper water of the stream. I immediately looked down at the rod. It was bent in the same, tight arc—miraculously, the bass was still on.

The moon was out now. It was low and full enough that its beam shone directly on Sheila there ahead of me in the canoe, washing her in a creamy, luminous glow. I could see the lithe, easy shape of her figure. I could see the way her hair curled down off her shoulders, the proud, alert tilt of her head, and all these things were as a tug on my heart. Not just Sheila, but the aura she carried about her of parties and casual touchings and grace. Behind me, I could feel the strain of the bass, steadier now, growing weaker, and this was another tug on my heart, not just the bass but the beat of the river and the slant of the stars and the smell of the night, until finally it seemed I would be torn apart between longings, split in half. Twenty yards ahead of us was the road, and once I pulled the canoe up on shore, the bass would be gone, irretrievably gone. If instead I stood up, grabbed the rod and started pumping, I would have it—as tired as the bass was, there was no chance it could get away. I reached down for the rod, hesitated, looked up to where Sheila was stretching herself lazily toward the sky, her small breasts rising beneath the soft fabric of her dress, and the tug was too much for me, and quicker than it takes to write down, I pulled a penknife from my pocket and cut the line in half.

With a sick, nauseous feeling in my stomach, I saw the rod unbend.

"My legs are sore," Sheila whined. "Are we there yet?"

Through a superhuman effort of self-control, I was able to beach the canoe and help Sheila off. The rest of the night is much foggier. We walked to the fair—there was the smell of
245 popcorn, the sound of guitars. I may have danced once or twice with her, but all I really remember is her coming over to me once the music was done to explain that she would be going home in Eric Caswell's Corvette.

"Okay," I mumbled.
250 For the first time that night she looked at me, really looked at me.

"You're a funny kid, you know that?"

Funny. Different. Dreamy. Odd. How many times was I to hear that in the years to come, all spoken with the same quizzi-
255 cal, half-accusatory tone Sheila used then. Poor Sheila! Before the month was over, the spell she cast over me was gone, but the memory of that lost bass haunted me all summer and haunts me still. There would be other Sheila Mants in my life, other fish, and though I came close once or twice, it was these
260 secret, hidden tuggings in the night that claimed me, and I never made the same mistake again.

[1983]

Understanding the Story

1. What made seventeen-year-old Sheila Mant so irre-
   sistibly attractive to the narrator during the summer he
   was fourteen?

2. Why did the narrator's mother disapprove of Sheila's
   family? How does the narrator's family seem to be different from the Mants? (What does it suggest, for example, that in the narrator's family, the dog is named for
   the heroine of a famous nineteenth-century Italian
   opera?)

3. What is the irony in the following statements? That is,
   what do they show about Sheila that the adult narrator
   and the reader understand but the fourteen-year-old boy
   didn't understand?

   a. "I'm playing outfield," she said. "I don't like the
      responsibility of having a base." (lines 56–57)

b. "You have a car?" she said, without looking up. (line 64)

(At fourteen, the narrator was two years too young for a driver's license.)

c. I was there ten minutes before Sheila appeared. (line 96)

4. What more does the reader learn about Sheila from her words and actions in the canoe? How does her reference to Eric Caswell (line 117), together with her desire to be driven in a car, foreshadow (give the reader a hint about) the ending of the story?

5. On his longed-for date with Sheila, the boy also caught "the biggest bass [he] had ever hooked" (lines 150–51). Why wasn't he pleased?

6. As they approached the shore, what caused the first "tug on [the boy's] heart" (line 222)? Which of the five senses—sight, hearing, touch, taste, or smell—were part of the appeal of each tug?

7. Explain the final sentence of the story.

a. What does the narrator mean by "other Sheila Mants" and "other fish"?

b. What does he mean by "these secret, hidden tuggings"?

c. What does he mean by "I never made the same mistake again"?

Developing a Way with Words

1. Much of the story's humor comes from the double point of view—the voice of the fourteen-year-old boy that the narrator once was contrasted with the man that he is at the time of telling the story. Which point of view is represented in each of the following comments?

a. I suppose to these jaded twenty-year-olds she seemed the incarnation of innocence and youth. (lines 29–31)

b. Finishing, I would boost myself up onto our dock and glance casually over toward her, but she was never watching, and the miraculous day she was, I immediately climbed the diving board and did my best tuck and a half for her, and continued diving until she had left and the sun went down and my longing was like a madness and I couldn't stop. (lines 36–41)

c. When I wasn't swimming laps to impress Sheila, I was back in our driveway practicing casts, and when I wasn't practicing casts, I was tying the line to Tosca, our springer spaniel, to test the reel's drag, and when I wasn't doing any of those things, I was fishing the river for bass. (lines 77–81)

d. Was her father a fisherman? Her antipathy toward fishing nothing more than normal filial rebellion? Had she tried it once? A messy encounter with worms? It doesn't matter. (lines 129–31)

2. In the following sentences, explain the figures of speech in dark type. Which of the five senses does each of them appeal to?

a. . . . the only part I remember clearly is emerging from the woods . . . **as bashful and frightened as a unicorn.** (lines 46–48)

b. Even by day the river was quiet, . . . , and at night it was a solitude difficult to believe, **a corridor of hidden life that ran between banks like a tunnel.** (lines 88–91)

c. The line, tightly coiled, peeled off the spool with **the shrill, tearing zip of a high-speed drill.** (lines 147–48)

d. I could have **threaded the eye of a needle** with the canoe, but the pull on the stern threw me off . . . . (lines 209–11)

Making Connections

1. The narrator says that the details of "the tortured will-I's, won't-I's, the agonized indecision over what to say, the false starts toward her house and embarrassed retreats" have been "seared from [his] memory" (lines 43–46)?

Would the story have been stronger if the author had provided some of those details, or can the reader perhaps fill them in from personal experience?

2. When the narrator had the bass on the line but didn't want to tell Sheila about it, how was his situation similar to the Asian expression "having a tiger by the tail"?

3. What do you think the narrator means when he says that "through a superhuman effort of self-control" (line 242), he was able to get both the canoe and Sheila safely up on shore? What did he want to do that he kept himself from doing?

4. From the evidence in the story, what were Sheila's dreams that summer? Why do you suppose she saw the boy as "a funny kid" (line 252)?

5. Nowadays, are cars as important to a young man's social success as they were at the time of this story?

6. If you had been the boy, would you have gone for the fish or the girl? Why? Have you ever tried to get two things when you could have settled for one and then ended up losing both?

7. How is the fourteen-year-old boy in this story like and unlike fourteen-year-old Chato in "The Somebody" by Danny Santiago?

Fine Points

"A few years
earlier, it might
have been
possible for me to
find the necessary
thrill simply in
going out with
white boys, the
forbidden fruit of
my mother's
generation; . . . ."

Fine Points

Andrea Lee
(born 1953)

Andrea Lee is one of the few black American authors who has presented the black middle class in fiction. A graduate of Harvard University, Lee is a staff writer for *The New Yorker* magazine, reporting on European topics from Milan, Italy, where she lives with her husband. Lee's first book, *Russian Journal* (1981), was based on her diary of the year that she and her husband spent in Moscow, where he had a graduate fellowship. The American couple's many contacts with Soviet young people gave them, as Lee said in 1981, "a view of life in Moscow and Leningrad that was very different from that of the diplomats and journalists we knew."

Lee's second book, the prize-winning *Sarah Phillips* (1984), is a collection of short stories originally published in *The New Yorker.* Together, the stories form an episodic novel and fictional autobiography. Like Andrea Lee, Sarah Phillips has grown up in comfortable circumstances in Philadelphia, attending private schools and enjoying social and academic success in the white world of her peers. In this privileged world, Sarah is able to distance herself from the more serious aspects of racial differences. She enjoys being seen as "exotic" because of her dark skin and she ignores the issues raised by the Civil Rights Movement of the 1960s, in which her parents have been active.

In "Fine Points," Sarah is in her third year at Radcliffe College, a distinguished institution of higher learning with close ties to Harvard University. (At the time of the story, 1973, Radcliffe admitted only women and Harvard College, the undergraduate division of the university, admitted only men; they have adjacent campuses in Cambridge, Massachusetts.) In the story, Lee uses real places: the "houses" (large dormitories with suites of rooms) where Harvard undergraduate men live; Harvard Yard, the lawn surrounded by the school's oldest buildings; Cambridge Common, a large city park between the Radcliffe and Harvard campuses; and the Café Pamplona, where members of the Harvard community still spend long hours talking over tiny cups of strong Italian coffee. Central Square, where Sarah's teacher Geoffrey Knacker lives, is a less expensive, less fashionable part of Cambridge.

The story is marked by irony, a contrast between the expected and the actual, the apparent and the real. The central dramatic irony is that Sarah (the narrator) and her roommate, who are intellectually gifted and socially privileged young women, want more than anything to be wicked women of the world. Why do you suppose they feel that way? What might they do to show their immorality? How good a chance do they have of realizing their desire on a college campus? What will the "fine points" of the title refer to?

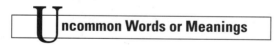
Uncommon Words or Meanings

fine ("It's a question of *fine* points.")—subtle or precise.

jeune fille ("a sexy *jeune fille* air worthy of Claudine")—(French) "young girl," suggesting youthful innocence.

Claudine ("worthy of *Claudine*")—the heroine of four novels by the early twentieth-century French writer Colette.

understated ("always trying to look *understated*")—deliberately simple.

the *Advocate* ("for an *Advocate* meeting")—the Harvard undergraduate literary magazine.

loftily ("I would retort *loftily*")—in a proud or superior manner.

busty ("the *bustiest Playboy* Playmates")—with large breasts, full-figured.

Donne, Herbert ("reading *Donne* and *Herbert* for seminar")—John Donne and George Herbert, seventeenth-century English metaphysical poets known for their elaborate images.

in concert ("We yearned, *in concert*")—in agreement, harmoniously.

a Gothic novel ("an array of *Gothic-novel* types")—a literary form characterized by horror, violence, and supernatural effects, often set in an isolated castle.

Brontëesque ("a positively *Brontëesque* conception of the ideal man")—in the style of the nineteenth-century English novelists who created dark, handsome, and masterful heroes in *Jane Eyre* (Charlotte Brontë) and *Wuthering Heights* (Emily Brontë).

a liaison ("envisioned *liaisons* with millionaires")—an illicit sexual relationship.

an upper ("moody filmmakers addicted to *uppers*")—(slang) a pharmaceutical drug that speeds up the metabolism and keeps a person awake.

to cut a dash ("were to *cut any dash* at all")—(British idiom) to be exciting and stylish in appearance and behavior.

to angle ("*angling* for members of the faculty")—to fish.

snappish ("grew *snappish* when I refused the loan")—bad-tempered, irritable.

to hide one's light under a bushel ("if I *hid my light under a bushel*, I wouldn't even get him to kiss me")—(idiom) to be modest about one's good qualities.

a thrift shop ("high heels I had bought in a *thrift shop*")—a store that sells second-hand clothing.

Hopalong Cassidy ("*Hopalong Cassidy* was the name we had privately given my boyfriend.")—the cowboy creation of actor William Boyd, first in films and comic books then in an enormously successful TV series of the 1950s, when Sarah was a child.

the bells desk ("behind the *bells desk* in the dormitory")—at the time of the story, the reception desk in a Radcliffe dormitory.

psychedelic ("a Volvo plastered with *psychedelic* stickers")—having vivid colors and distorted shapes that suggest drug-created hallucinations or distortions of perception.

stoned ("Hopalong had gotten very *stoned* at the Dartmouth game")—(slang) in an artificially (drug-) induced euphoric state.

Dartmouth ("at the *Dartmouth* game")—Dartmouth competes with Harvard and the other Ivy League colleges in sports.

the Temptations ("the *Temptations'* song 'My Girl'")—a black male quartet, popularizers of the "Motown sound" in the early 1960s.

a townie ("where Cambridge *townies* liked to hang around smoking dope")—(slang) a college-age person who lives in a college town but is not a college student.

dope ("hang around smoking *dope*")—(slang) here, marijuana or hashish, though the term can include other drugs.

Anna Karenina ("I felt a bit like *Anna Karenina*")—in Leo Tolstoy's nineteenth-century novel, a married woman who has an illicit love affair with a dashing younger man.

to give (something) a wide berth ("*giving a wide berth* to the monument")—(idiom) to stay as far away as possible from (something).

Jimi Hendrix ("a guy who looked like *Jimi Hendrix*")—a black guitarist and singer of the1960s who sported a wild Afro hairdo and psychedelic clothing.

"The Flea" ("I recited a poem to my invisible companion—Donne's *'The Flea'*")—a clever seduction poem by John Donne.

comp lit ("just like a coffee date with any callow *comp lit* major")—comparative literature.

to drop ("suggesting we *drop* mescaline")—(slang) to swallow a drug.

mescaline ("drop *mescaline*")—a drug that acts as a stimulant.

a dissertation ("finished my *dissertation* three years ago")—the last step in earning a doctoral degree, which is usually necessary for a full-time teaching appointment in a four-year college.

muted ("one of those *muted* social disasters")—quiet, softened.

L. L. Bean ("trudged off in his *L. L. Bean* boots")—a famous Maine sporting goods store.

Christopher Robin ("nicknamed him *Christopher Robin*")—the young boy in A. A. Milne's early twentieth-century Winnie-the-Pooh stories.

grass ("an ounce of *grass* that he'd just bought")—(slang) marijuana.

an epiphany ("The woman of *epiphanies*")—a moment of enlightenment when an underlying truth suddenly becomes clear.

the [Rolling] Stones ("dancing to a *Stones* tape")—the famous British rock-and-roll group that debuted in 1964.

a post-doc ("a *post-doc* a bit older than Geoffrey Knacker")—a person doing research at a university on a post-doctoral fellowship.

to flutter hearts ("*fluttered hearts* all through the chem labs")—to make hearts beat faster with romantic excitement.

Buffalo Bill ("a *Buffalo Bill* mustache")—William F. Cody, a nineteenth-century American frontier scout and showman who sported a wide, bushy mustache.

Techie ("a *Techie* grape-juice concoction")—(slang) created by a "Techie," a student at the Massachusetts Institute of Technology (MIT).

to lace ("a Techie grape-juice concoction *laced* with acid")—to add a small amount of a stronger substance to a drink.

acid ("laced with *acid*")—LSD, a drug that produces hallucinations.

One great thing about Margaret was that she wore exactly the same size clothing that I did, an excellent quality in a roommate; she had, however, completely different taste, with an inclination toward plunging necklines, crimson tights, and minidresses in big, bold Scandinavian prints. My own wardrobe ran to jeans and black turtlenecks, odd little somber-colored tunics that I felt made me look like a wood nymph, and short pleated skirts that seemed to me to convey a sexy *jeune fille* air worthy of Claudine at school. "You literary types are always trying to look understated," Margaret would say whenever she saw me dressed for seminar, for an *Advocate* meeting, or for a date. She was a chemistry major from Wellesley, Massachusetts, an avid lacrosse player with a terrific figure and a pair of unabashed blue eyes that revealed a forceful, stubborn nature—Margaret could keep an argument going for days. She adored fresh air and loathed reticence and ambiguity, and she had little patience with a roommate who, languid from lack of exercise, spent weeks reworking a four-word line of poetry.

"It's a question of fine points," I would retort loftily, though I had only a vague idea of what that might mean.

Margaret and I got along well for young women with such different souls. We spent a lot of time together in our cramped dormitory suite, squabbling comfortably over clothes and discussing romance—the one subject on which we were, to some extent, in agreement. The suite was on the fourth floor of Currier House; it consisted of two tiny rooms, a bathroom we'd decorated for a giggle with pinups of the bustiest *Playboy* Playmates we could find, and a kitchenette filled with moldy oranges stolen from the cafeteria. Our windows faced east, toward the corner of Garden and Linnaean streets—a lovely view, really, with the Observatory woods, the flat-bottomed, whale-shaped clouds that came sailing down from Maine, and the tall, somber Cambridge houses back of the trees.

In the winter of 1973, our junior year at Harvard, on afternoons when Margaret was back from the lab and I was supposed to be at my desk reading Donne and Herbert for seminar or writing poetry for Professor Hawks's versification class, we would hang out in Margaret's room and drink oolong tea, which Margaret brewed so black it became a kind of solvent. Lounging on Margaret's bed, below a periodic table she'd tacked up on the wall, we'd complain at length about our boyfriends. These young men, a couple of blameless seniors from Adams and Dunster Houses, were certainly ardent and attentive, but they bored us because they seemed appropriate. We yearned, in concert, to replace them with unsuitable men— an array of Gothic-novel types who didn't seem at all hackneyed to Margaret and me. (Margaret, the scientist, had in fact a positively Brontëesque conception of the ideal man.) We envisioned liaisons with millionaires the age of our fathers, with alcoholic journalists, with moody filmmakers addicted to uppers; Margaret's particular thing was depraved European nobility. A few years earlier it might have been possible for me to find the necessary thrill simply in going out with white boys, the forbidden fruit of my mother's generation; but in the arty circles I frequented at Harvard, such pairings were just about required, if one was to cut any dash at all.

What our fantasies boiled down to was that Margaret and I, in the age-old female student tradition, ended up angling for members of the faculty.

"It's just a question of days before Dr. Bellemere tumbles," said Margaret one afternoon. (She flirted shamelessly with her adviser, but for some reason could not bring herself to call him by his first name—Don.) "And *then*, what naughty delights!"

As a matter of fact, I was the one who first was offered the chance to taste those delights. In February a genuine instructor—Geoffrey Knacker, who had taught my seminar on metaphysical poetry the previous semester, and who shared an apartment in Central Square with Millicent Tunney, another junior faculty member—asked me to meet him for a cup of coffee. Margaret sat cross-legged on my bed while I got dressed for the date—we were to meet at six at the Café Pamplona— and grew snappish when I refused the loan of a pair of red tights. She told me that if I hid my light under a bushel, I wouldn't even get him to kiss me. I didn't listen to her. I was busy making myself look as beautiful and mysterious as I could, and when I had slicked my hair back into a bun, rimmed my eyes with dark pencil, and put on a severe gray dress with

a pair of black high heels I had bought in a thrift shop, even
80 Margaret had to applaud the result.

"If Hopalong calls, tell him I'm riding in the Tour de France," I said. Hopalong Cassidy was the name we had privately given my boyfriend, who had what I thought was an unnecessarily jaunty gait.

85 "You're a cold, hard thing," said Margaret in an approving tone.

I owned a rather rubbed-looking sealskin jacket that had belonged to my mother; when I had wrapped it around me, waved goodbye to the girl who stood studying behind the bells
90 desk of the dormitory, and stepped outside into the February twilight, I had an agreeable feeling of satisfaction about the way I looked, and an agitated romantic feeling about the meeting to come. "Perhaps I'm in love," I thought, though in fact I could barely remember what Geoffrey Knacker looked like.

95 It was ten minutes to six. I walked down Garden Street toward Cambridge Common, listening to the unaccustomed click of my high heels on the brick sidewalk, slippery with melted snow and patches of dirty ice. In the darkness around me, students riding bicycles or walking with book bags were
100 returning to dinner from classes in Harvard Yard. The sky over the dark buildings and narrow streets was a deep lustrous blue, streaked at the edges with pinkish light, and the air was cold and damp. Near Follen Street a small battered Datsun was trying unsuccessfully to park between a jacked-up Riviera
105 and a Volvo plastered with psychedelic stickers. The sound of grinding gears made me think of the time during my sophomore year when a precursor of my boyfriend Hopalong had gotten very stoned at the Dartmouth game and had pursued me along Garden Street by backing up his car for a whole
110 block, all the while declaiming the words from the Temptations' song "My Girl." The incident had infuriated me at the time, but now I thought of it as something gay and romantic, the sort of thing that happened constantly to a woman destined to exercise a fatal influence upon men.

115 My feeling of agitation increased as I approached the Common. The usual shouts and guffaws were coming from the war monument in the middle, where Cambridge townies liked to hang around smoking dope and drinking wine, but they seemed far away. I looked through the rows of leafless maples at the

120 university towers and traffic lights clustering ahead of me, and felt an unreasonable, blissful happiness to be walking in high heels and a fur coat on a clear evening to a meeting with a man who was likely to mean trouble—the kind of trouble that mothers and magazine articles particularly warned against. I felt a

125 bit like Anna Karenina, burning with a sinful glow; and as if someone beside me in the darkness had spoken a few passionate, muted words, it seemed to me that I was ravishingly beautiful. I began to pretend that someone *was* walking with me: a lover who didn't resemble my boyfriend, or even Geoffrey

130 Knacker. This imaginary lover, in fact, didn't have much of any appearance at all, only a compelling simplicity of character that granted every dangerous wish I had ever had. As I walked through the Common, giving a wide berth to the monument, where two long-haired girls were giggling beside a guy who

135 looked like Jimi Hendrix, I crooked my fingers very slightly inside the pocket of my fur jacket, as if I were holding hands with someone. And then I did something I never afterward admitted to anyone, not even Margaret: I recited a poem to my invisible companion—Donne's "The Flea."

140 By the time I got to the Pamplona, I had almost forgotten Geoffrey Knacker, who rose from his tiny table to greet me, with an air of being slightly startled by my appearance. He was a tall, thin man with a mournful, rather handsome face and gray half-moons of skin under his eyes; in the white-tiled, low-

145 ceilinged interior of the Pamplona, surrounded by graduate students chatting over cappuccino, he appeared curiously yellowish and misanthropic, as if he'd lived most of his life in a remote tropical outpost. He helped me with my coat, and I ordered an ice cream. Then the two of us began to talk, rather

150 constrainedly, about metaphysical poetry until Geoffrey began paying me heavy-handed compliments.

"I always felt that behind your reserved manner in class was a rare sensitivity of nature," he said, giving me a slow, gloomy smile, and I, who had been attracted by just that smile

155 in the seminar, found myself filled not with rapture but with an inexplicable annoyance. It occurred to me that this meeting was just like a coffee date with any callow comp lit major, who would begin by throwing out portentous hints about his ideal woman and end, ritually, by suggesting we drop mescaline and

160 swim nude in the Adams House pool. I tried to think of the

romantic fact that Geoffrey Knacker was an instructor, and that both of us were flouting lovers in order to meet, but all I could seem to feel was irritation at a flat, straw-colored mole that Geoffrey had where his jaw met his neck, and at the way
165 that as he talked, he joined the tips of his fingers together and pumped them in and out in a tiny bellowslike motion. We were sitting at an inconspicuous table in a corner, but it seemed to me, in my hypersensitive state, that all the other students in the Pamplona could see the mole and the working fingertips,
170 and were laughing discreetly at them.

As I rattled my spoon in my ice-cream dish, some demon prompted me to say, "But certainly you must have seen hundreds of exceptional students in all your years as a teacher.

"Hundreds?" repeated Geoffrey Knacker in an injured tone.
175 "Why, no, I finished my dissertation three years ago. I am only thirty-one."

We didn't really have much to say to each other. It was clear, in fact, that our original attraction had become puzzling and abortive, and that this meeting was one of those muted
180 social disasters that can be devastating if one cares. I didn't care much; nor, it seemed, did Geoffrey Knacker. We shook hands and parted outside the Pamplona without even mentioning plans to get in touch. When he zipped up his jacket and, with one last unhappy smile, trudged off in his L. L. Bean boots
185 toward Central Square, I clicked off back to Radcliffe in my high heels, feeling positively elated. Geoffrey Knacker, I decided, was a bore, but the *fact* of Geoffrey Knacker was exciting. As I came into Harvard Square and threaded my way through the slush and evening traffic on Massachusetts Avenue,
190 the romantic sensation I'd had while walking through the Common returned to me in full force. I seemed, agreeably, to be taking up the strands of an interrupted idyll, and in my right palm, deep in the pocket of the fur jacket, was the pleasant tickling feeling that denoted the grasp of my imaginary lover.
195 When I got back to the suite, Margaret was working on a problem sheet for Chem 105, and her boyfriend—a young man with such an earnest, childlike gaze that we'd nicknamed him Christopher Robin—was seated cross-legged on her bed, using a metal mesh contraption to sift seeds and stems out of an
200 ounce of grass he'd just bought. (One of Margaret's complaints about him was his methodical attitude toward sex and drugs.)

"Oo-la-la—very thirties," said Christopher Robin, giving my outfit the old once-over, and then Margaret dragged me into the bathroom.

205   "Well, what happened?" she demanded, locking the door, turning on both faucets, and settling herself on the sink counter under the enormous bosom of one of the Playmates we'd pinned up. "He must have kissed you—or did you fall into bed together? You're absolutely beaming."

210   "Knacker was actually kind of a fizzle," I said. "But it was fun anyway."

"Idiot child," said Margaret. "Take off that coat—you've wasted it. I knew you should have worn red stockings."

When I tried to explain myself, she leaned back against the
215   bathroom mirror, closed her eyes, and giggled so that the frame of the mirror shook. "My artistic roommate," she said. "The woman of epiphanies. You're going to kill me with your fine points."

A few weeks later Margaret was dancing to a Stones tape
220   at a party in a converted airplane factory up near MIT when she ran into her adviser, Dr. Bellemere, whom she at last succeeded in calling Don. Bellemere, who was a post-doc a bit older than Geoffrey Knacker, and who fluttered hearts all through the chem labs with his leather vest and Buffalo Bill
225   mustache, had had a lot of the punch, which was a Techie grape-juice concoction laced with acid. He led Margaret out of the strobe lights into a dark corner of the loft, kissed her passionately, and told her he spent every lab session thinking about her legs. A triumph for Margaret—except that she inex-
230   plicably discovered a preference for Christopher Robin, and so the thing with Bellemere went no further, except for a bit of embarrassment in lab.

"But there was something really solid there—a kiss, not just daydreams," Margaret told me pointedly when we dis-
235   cussed it later. For a change, we were sitting among the scattered books and papers of my room, while I packed my book bag to go down and visit Hopalong at Adams House.

"I don't think the two situations were so different," I said. "I'm afraid, sweetheart, that whatever we try to do, in our two
240   different ways, we end up being just a couple of nice girls."

"Oh, I hope not!" said Margaret, flopping backward on the bed. "But anyway," she went on stubbornly after a minute, " a real kiss is better than an imaginary one.

And she thumped her booted feet on my bedspread for
245 emphasis.

I wanted to contradict her, but then I remembered how
bullheaded and tenacious Margaret could be in an argument,
how tiresomely withholding of her oolong tea and the little
English butter biscuits that her mother sent her, and that I
250 loved. In the end I just raised my eyebrows with the air of one
to whom has been granted higher knowledge, and kept my
mouth shut.

[1984]

Understanding the Story

1. Sarah, the narrator, says that she and her roommate
   "got along well for young women with such different
   souls" (lines 22–23).

   a. What are some of the specific ways that they are spiri-
      tually different from each other?

   b. In what ways are they alike? For example, what
      details suggest that they are both highly intelligent
      young women from well-to-do families?

2. Why were Sarah and Margaret dissatisfied with their
   Harvard boyfriends? What was "hackneyed" about their
   vision of the "ideal man" (lines 47–49)? Was their solu-
   tion to the problem original or was it also hackneyed?

3. Sarah's date with Geoffrey Knacker provides fine examples of irony, with a contrast between what is expected
   and how things turn out in the first two examples and a
   contrast between what is said and what is implied in the
   third example.

   a. What were the romantic elements of the narrator's
      fifteen-minute walk from her dorm to the Café Pam-
      plona? What were the unromantic elements?

   b. How well did the reality of Geoffrey Knacker match
      Sarah's romantic imagination? From what we can
      guess, how well did Sarah match Geoffrey Knacker's
      idea of what she would be like on a date?

c. In the comment that Sarah says "some demon" (line 171) prompted her to make, what was Sarah implying about Geoffrey Knacker?

4. Why, when Geoffrey Knacker had been such a disappointment, did Sarah feel "positively elated" (line 186) on her way back home? That is, what was the "epiphany" (line 217) that Margaret later teased her about?

5. How was Margaret's experience with Don Bellemere (lines 219–32) like and unlike Sarah's date with Geoffrey Knacker?

6. Why do you suppose Sarah didn't agree that "a real kiss is better than an imaginary one" (lines 242–43)? How does this philosophical disagreement reflect the difference in the roommates' academic interests?

7. Sarah says that spending weeks rewriting a four-word line of poetry was "a question of fine points" (line 20). Margaret returns to the same words when she says, "You're going to kill me with your fine points" (lines 217–18). What do you suppose each of them means? How are their comments related to the title of the story?

Developing a Way with Words

1. In the following comments, what is the denotation (the dictionary meaning) and connotation (the emotional implication) of each of the words or phrases in dark type?

   a. **white boys,** the **forbidden fruit** of my mother's generation (lines 54–55)

   b. "It's just a question of days before Dr. Bellemere **tumbles.** . . . And *then* what **naughty** delights." (lines 61–64)

   c. I was the one who first was offered the chance to **taste** those **delights.** (lines 65–66)

2. The range of vocabulary in this story is a remarkable mix of literary terms and campus slang, including terms associated with the drug culture of the sixties and seventies. Divide the following words from the story into four lists: "Literary References," "Popular Culture," "Collegiate Slang," and "Drug-Related Slang":

> acid, Anna Karenina, Brontëesque, Buffalo Bill, Christopher Robin, Claudine, comp lit, Donne, dope, a Gothic novel, grass, Hopalong Cassidy, Jimi Hendrix, L. L. Bean, metaphysical poetry, a post-doc, psychedelic, stoned, the Rolling Stones, a Techie, the Temptations, a townie, an upper

What is the effect of mixing the different kinds of words?

M aking Connections

1. From what you have observed, is Sarah accurate in describing "angling for members of the faculty" as "an age-old female student tradition" (lines 59–60)? Do you think it is proper for students to flirt with faculty members? For faculty members to date their students?

2. What did the young women accomplish by giving their boyfriends private nicknames? Have you ever had a private nickname for someone you were going out with? Do you have a private nickname for any of your teachers?

3. Have you ever had a romantic longing for someone that ended as soon as the person showed signs of romantic interest in you?

4. Have you had the occasion to live away from home with one or more roommates? If so, what are the similarities between your roommate situation and that in the story? What are the differences?

5. There are many references to the drug culture of the 1960s. From the evidence in the story, what was the

attitude toward drug use among upper-middle class students at intellectually demanding colleges? From your knowledge, what is the current attitude toward drug use among college students?

6. "Fine Points" takes place forty or more years after Ernest Hemingway's "Hills Like White Elephants." How are Sarah in "Fine Points" and Jig in Hemingway's story different in their attitudes toward their boyfriends? What factors might account for the differences: the time of the story? the sex of the author? the women's level of education? their race? something else?

7. Like W. D. Wetherell's "The Bass, the River, and Sheila Mant," this story is told by an adult reporting on a time when he or she was much younger. What else do the two stories have in common? What are some of the ways in which they are different?

Where You Have Been, Where You Are Going

"'How long were you in jail?' I ask through everyone's laughter. Grandfather keeps an even expression."

Where You Have Been, Where You Are Going

Mark Steven Hess
(born 1966)

Mark Steven Hess has lived nearly all his life on Colorado's vast High Plains, east of Denver. In high school, he was interested mostly in science until his senior year, when he wrote a short story that impressed his English teacher, who had just published a first novel. "I'd hate to suggest this to anyone," the teacher said, "but why don't you try writing?"

Hess took the advice, finding time to write during the summers. He also became a high school English teacher in Brush, Colorado, one hundred miles northeast of Denver. The school enrolls four hundred students, some of whom travel forty or more miles a day to attend classes. Sports are important in the school, so besides teaching, Hess coaches the Brush "Beetdiggers" teams in boys' and girls' track and girls' basketball. Hess offers this report on how the name came to be:

"School legend has it that the name 'Beetdiggers' was chosen in a contest in the 1940s. The prize for the winning student was to be a used car. Now, the basketball team's star player was a country kid who had no way to get home after practice and so was going to have to quit the team. What would you do in a case like that? At Brush High School, it was silently agreed that whatever name this player chose would win the contest. The rest is history."

"Where You Have Been, Where You Are Going"—Hess's first published story—was chosen for the 1989 volume of

The Best of the West: New Short Stories from the Wide Side of the Mississippi. "The story really came out my love for Colorado's High Plains," the author says. "When you stand on the open prairie, you get the sense that you're incredibly alone. Recently, irrigation has turned the High Plains into beautiful farmland, but there are still many places out here almost untouched by humans—miles and miles of prairie and sage that could just swallow you up."

Within that context of isolation, Hess dramatizes ways that connections are made between generations. He also reminds us that in the American West, as in other "uncharted" parts of the world, the "tall tale"—like those told by the grandfather in this story—became the way explorers described the wonders they had seen to open-mouthed audiences back home. Like the land that provides its setting, this story rises and falls between different time periods. (Extra space between paragraphs signals the shift from one time to another.) In the first time period ("today"), the narrator retraces the steps of a walk in his childhood. In the second time period (forty years earlier), he relives the day of that walk. In the third time period (forty-one years earlier), he remembers the time he met his grandfather and a story that the grandfather told. In the fourth time period (more than forty-one years earlier), the grandfather's story takes place. (This flashback technique—having a character remember a past event which the audience then sees—is familiar from movies.) As the title suggests, we must remember the past in order to understand the present and anticipate the future.

Uncommon Words or Meanings

a rest home ("died seven miles away in a *rest home*")—a residence for older people who need housekeeping services (meals, sheets and towels, laundry) but not extensive medical treatment.

to knead ("He *kneaded* my shoulder.")—to massage firmly.

lather ("brushing thick *lather* onto his face")—a soapy foam used to soften a man's beard before he shaves.

girl-craziest ("one of the *girl-craziest* persons")—romantically excited by girls; when said to a four-year-old boy, this is a form of good-natured teasing.

a swell ("The ruts lead up and down the *swells* of the prairie")—(1) a gradual rise in ground level; (2) a long wave that moves without breaking; in the story, the prairie is described in terms of the ocean.

a homestead ("the old *homestead*")—in the nineteenth-century United States, land granted by a state government to any settler who would build a home, dig a well for water, and clear and farm the land.

an arrowhead ("Indians and *arrowheads*")—a piece of stone, one or two inches in length, chipped to make a pointed tip for an arrow.

to pee ("he has to *pee*")—(informal) to urinate.

Papoose, Squaw, Hermoso ("he could name all the tribes, Sioux, Cheyenne, *Papoose, Squaw, Hermoso*")—American Indian words for "baby" (*papoose*) and "woman" (*squaw*) and the Spanish word for "beautiful" (*hermoso*); only "Sioux" and "Cheyenne" are real tribal names.

even ("keeps an *even* expression")—unchanging.

a teepee ("had set up a *teepee*")—a cone-shaped tent made of buffalo hide.

a bird dog (his *bird dog* Scooter")—a dog used to hunt game birds.

a kick ("the *kick* of the old shotgun")—the jerk backwards of a gun when it is fired.

fed up ("the Indians got more than *fed up* with all this")—annoyed, out of patience.

walking on water ("*running on top of the water* just like Jesus Christ")—the miracle of Jesus walking on the waters of the Sea of Galilee is described in Matthew 14:25.

to swivel ("*swiveling* around faster than a weather cock")—to turn or spin quickly on a single point.

a weather cock ("faster than a *weather cock*")—a thin plate of wood or metal that turns to indicate the direction of the wind, often in the shape of a male chicken (a "cock").

sod ("the *sod* house")—a grass-covered piece of earth held together by roots; in the U.S., used for home-building by early white settlers on the Great Plains, where there were very few trees.

lye ("how Grandma used to make *lye* soap")—a strong chemical substance (sodium hydroxide), obtained by passing water through wood ashes; American pioneer women combined lye with animal fat to make soap for washing clothes.

I shut the door of my car. I can hardly hear the noise it makes. All sounds are sifted here, broken up by the prairie, digested and dispersed in fine pieces through the air. The color is brown—brown plains of brown dirt, brown weeds rolling off
5 north, south, east, west with a brown road slashing across them. The sky contains no clouds. It is a solid blue sheet meeting brown prairie in one straight line as if someone had pasted two pieces of colored paper together.

I walk north across a ditch, and I thank God this is not my
10 home.

This is my grandfather's home. He was born here. He spent his life here before he died seven miles away in a rest home in a town called Arickeree. There are five paved streets in that town, each lined with elm trees on both sides. It looks like an
15 oasis as you approach it from the state highway—122 miles straight east of Denver by counting mile markers. When you get there, though, you can see that the trees are only a cover for more brown—brown-faced people with lines of brown underneath their fingernails from working in their brown yards.
20 I only saw my grandfather once. I was four years old. One day an old man appeared in our house. Dad said, "Son, this is your grandfather." The old man shook my hand and laughed. He slapped my back. He kneaded my shoulder. He wrestled me close to him and squeezed my knee until I squirmed and
25 laughed and wrestled his big hand to get loose and finally he could say, "You're just about one of the girl-craziest persons I ever seen."

He stayed only for a week, and when he left I kept expecting to see him still in our house. I thought I'd see him just around
30 the corner in the hallway, smoking cigarettes at night in his bedroom, or brushing thick lather onto his face as he whistled to himself in front of the bathroom mirror. I have never seen a man since who has whistled so often or so well.

I continue north now, keeping to the right tire rut—the same
35 rut Dad and I followed to the old homestead I have only seen once before. The ruts lead up and down the swells of the prairie

to the homestead. Each swell is like a tiny horizon, and there are places where the swells are so abrupt and so close together that I do not know what is ahead of me thirty yards away. When I walk I feel as if I am climbing ocean waves. I am surrounded by waves, and though the waves don't move, I still feel threatened. I walk on. I walk on because I know that soon I will rise up over a swell and there will be the windmill—there will be the lighthouse that tells me the homestead is not far away.

It is forty years before. Grandfather has just died. I am five years old. After the funeral Dad stops at a store with a green-and-white-striped awning. We go inside and there Dad buys me a pair of black cowboy boots. I wear the boots out of the store and run down the street to try them out. They are exactly the kind I want. "Yes," Dad says, satisfied, "those are very fine boots."

Dad says he wants to show me something. We get in the car and drive on dirt roads. On the way, Dad tells me of Indians and arrowheads and how he used to go hunting arrowheads after big rainstorms when the dust on the ground was newly melted away by the drops of rain. By the time Dad stops the car, my feet have begun to sweat in the leather boots. This can't be what he wants to show me because there is nothing here. I guess he has to pee. He gets out of the car and motions for me to follow. He takes my hand, and we walk north along tire ruts. "Just watch for the windmill," he says. "When you see the windmill we'll be there." We are going to see where my grandfather grew up, a place where there were real cowboys and real Indians.

My grandfather stretches his legs out in front of him. He is a big man. He takes up two spaces on the sofa just getting comfortable. He tells us a story about a windmill.

The windmill has stopped turning. They have had no way to get water for three days. They try greasing the windmill; they try replacing the gears. Nothing works. Two Indians pass by. Grandfather offers them a shotgun and a pint of whiskey if they will make it rain. They ask why doesn't he just try greasing the windmill. Grandpa throws two extra pints of whiskey into the deal. Finally they accept. The Indians dance all night, and the next day it rains—a thunderstorm. Lightning strikes the wind-

75 mill, and the windmill begins to turn. It continues to rain for twelve days. No work gets done, and all the people around Arickeree get scared because they have never seen so much rain. The sheriff comes from Arickeree and arrests Grandfather for negligence in giving rain dancers too much whiskey.

80 Dad has dropped my hand. He walks looking straight ahead and does not notice me. Now and then I have to skip to keep up. "Can't we drive?" I ask. "Ain't no vehicle could make the trip over this land," he says. He is talking like Grandfather. The new boots hurt my feet. "Is it far?" "Not far." "Are we 85 almost there?" "Look for the windmill," he says. "Dad . . ." I say. I pause. I make him see me. "My feet hurt." He looks solemn, slightly hurt, slightly pleading. "We'll try going slower," he says.

He stops, points, and turns, indicating the horizon. "Right there," he says, "settlers used to come on covered wagons. It 90 wasn't easy out here. Sure there were Indians . . ."

"Indians?"

"Indians. And you had to watch out for them for too, but getting lost out here was just as dangerous. You might think it's hard getting lost in such an open place, but that's just the prob- 95 lem. There's nothing out here to look at to see if you're going in a straight line. And then there are these swells. You get down in between two swells and you can't see where you're going or where you've been. The only thing that can keep you going is hope and that next swell—hope that soon you'd come 100 over a swell and there would be a river you could follow, or maybe there would be the Rocky Mountains and you could head straight out to them."

"There was Indians here?" I ask, walking again, forgetting now my discomfort.

105 "Indians? Sure."

"Bad Indians?"

"Well, some were bad, I guess. But most of them your Grandpa knew were good."

"Grandpa knew Indians?"

110 "Sure. Don't you remember his stories? He knew as many Indians as you might ever want to know. He could name all the tribes, Sioux, Cheyenne, Papoose, Squaw, Hermoso. In fact . . . not far from here, just on the other side of your Grandpa's homestead, is an Indian grave."

115 "Can we see it?"

"Yes, I suppose a fellow could walk to it. No . . . it really isn't too far from here."

We walk faster.

There was the windmill, just above the horizon, pushing up
120 higher and higher over the next swell with each step as if it were growing up out of the prairie. I remember now the way I yelled the first I saw it, how I ran ahead of Dad and laughed, feeling like a real cowboy in my black cowboy boots. This day, though, calls for silence.
125 I walk, hands in my pockets. I feel my pocketknife there, cold, familiar. The knife has no color anymore, though it was once shiny gold, and the end of the longest blade is chipped off square from using it as a screwdriver. Every family has an heirloom—a sort of talisman. This knife is ours. Somehow . . . when
130 I touch it—when I fold my hand around it—I can feel Father's strong hands, and as I hold the knife now I do not want to let go.

I am certain that Dad must have been relieved, even satisfied that day with all my running and yelling as we approached the homestead. I am certain because I know what it is like to
135 lose your father. I am certain because even now I want someone to fill this place with laughter. If I could have any wish right now, it would be that I could fill this place myself.

"How long were you in jail?" I ask through everyone's laughter. Grandfather keeps an even expression. "It was two
140 weeks," he says, "two weeks and then the sheriff let me go." He talked while his fork rested on his plate. He talked with his fork poised in front of his mouth. He talked through mouthfuls of scalloped potatoes. He talked through bites of strawberry shortcake.
145 When Grandfather returned to the homestead he found the two Indians waiting for him. They had set up a teepee and had waited there two weeks for Grandfather for the sole purpose of learning from Grandfather how to operate the shotgun he had given them. There was never a time when it had rained for
150 twelve days before on the prairie. It was as if the ground didn't know what to do with all that water, so for a while the water just stayed there, and the prairie was dotted all over with small lakes. Grandfather wasn't going to let an opportunity like this

slip away, so he grabbed his shotgun and his bird dog Scooter
155 and took the Indians out to see if they might be able to hunt a
few of the ducks that flew in off the lakes.

Grandfather was a bit worried that Scooter might not quite
know what to do with a duck. Scooter had never seen a duck
before, nor a lake for that matter. But right away they saw
160 some ducks and one, two, Grandfather gets off two shots and
two ducks fall to the ground. Scooter brought the ducks back,
not even hesitating, and neither duck had so much as one
tooth mark on its body. Meanwhile the Indians were shooting
wildly with their shotgun and coming closer to killing them-
165 selves than any duck. One would shoot and the kick of the old
shotgun would knock him all the way to the ground. Before
that one had time to swear, the other one would grab the shotgun and fire. Then both Indians tried holding the shotgun at
the same time, but both barrels shot off and knocked both the
170 Indians to the ground. Pretty soon, the Indians got more than
fed up with this, and finally they asked Grandfather to come
along with them; they'd show him the real way to hunt ducks.

When they arrived at the next lake, the Indians walked up
close without any noise and crouched down low into their own
175 shadows. Now Grandfather can't figure out how the hell the
Indians are going to catch a duck this way, but soon the Indians start making sort of low and throaty duck noises with their
palms cupped over their mouths. Sure enough, within five minutes four or five ducks swim up close to the edge where the
180 Indians crouch. Suddenly one of the Indians springs into the
water and grabs a duck by the neck, twisting its head nearly
off before the duck has time to quack even once in surprise.

An hour of crouching, springing, and twisting passes before
the Indians relax. The result is a pile of a dozen ducks with bro-
185 ken necks lying on the ground beside the Indians. Grandfather
was so happy at this that he forgot himself for a moment and
shot a duck sitting on top of the water. He completely forgot
about Scooter and his ignorance about duck hunting and water.
Before Grandfather could do anything, though, Scooter was off
190 and running on top of the water just like Jesus Christ. Scooter
was there and back even before Grandfather had time tell him
he would drown, and just as always the hound laid the bird in
Grandfather's hand without a solitary tooth mark. From then
on the Indians never did get closer than a careful arm's length

to Scooter in fear that whatever demon that made the dog run on the water might suddenly let loose and jump inside one of them. Grandfather's brain was swiveling faster than a weather cock in a tornado, but he never let the Indians see he was affected. Later, though, when Grandpa got the chance to fill up a pipe and sit down to think, he worked it all out in his head. After then, he wasn't troubled anymore because it was all just a matter of finding a logical explanation. And it didn't take Grandpa too long to realize that the reason Scooter could walk right on top of the water like that was because Grandpa never did teach the dog how to swim, and the dog was too dumb to figure out for himself that trying to run on top of water was likely to result in drowning.

It is getting darker. The prairie is silver; the prairie is grey. We stand by the windmill. It is just an old windmill, nothing else. There are no lightning marks, no buffalo hides tacked to it. I don't know why we have to stay here so long. Perhaps dad sees more to this place than I do. Maybe he can still see what used to be here, the sod house, the turning windmill, my grandfather at the window, his face, his hands. I look at the windmill. I want to ask where the lightning struck it. I want to ask how it brings up water. I want to ask how long it will be until we can go to the Indian grave. But Dad does not notice me, so I turn sideways and try to make myself thinner. I don't want to get in the way.

Grandfather is wearing black cowboy boots that he and I polished the night before. He is boarding the bus that will take him back to Colorado. He shakes my hand. He tells me I have a strong hand. He slaps my back, kneads my shoulder, and then gets on the bus—black boots clunking up the steps.

Dad says we will have to hurry to make it to the Indian grave before dark. He starts east, each stride a mountain. I nearly have to run to keep up. At first I am eager, but it doesn't take too long for me to remember my boots. "My feet hurt," I say. Dad keeps striding. "It is only a little farther," he says. "But they really hurt," I say, letting a whine slip into my tone. "Watch the horizon," he says, "that next swell, maybe there will be that grave on the other side."
It does not work. I feel the blister anyway.

Dad is striding—flying—and I keep falling away, my arm getting longer, his hand holding tighter to mine until he is almost dragging me with him. Tears come now. My feet drag and stumble over the hard mounds of dirt. No wagon full of settlers can stop the tears; no promise of an Indian grave can keep me silent. I let the tears force my mouth to open, and I cry.

I reach to feel the pocketknife. For an instant my hand does not find it, and I imagine the knife already lost—already buried in the dust somewhere on the prairie. For an instant my body, neck, and head shrivel together, my trachea constricts and I cannot breathe; for an instant I want to let my body fall, fold together, and collapse on the prairie. But then I find it. I hold the knife tight in my hand and do not let go. It is my turn now to stand at the windmill and remember. Jesus . . . they were handsome men.

We are almost back to the car again. Dad carries me on his shoulders, my cowboy boots bouncing off his chest. Dad is striding still, now happily, now jokingly telling me stories of rattlesnakes, cowboys and cattle drives, and how Grandma used to make lye soap. I try not to be happy. I try not to smile, but it is no use. My tears are already dry.

Before we get into the car, Dad crouches low in front of me. In his hand is a pocketknife. He wants me to take it. In my hand the knife seems much larger. "I got that knife on my tenth birthday," he says. "Your grandfather gave it to me." I put the knife in my pocket, feeling on the outside to make sure it is safe there. We get in the car. I feel older now, grown up because I have my own knife. I look at my father and somehow he too is older.

"Dad," I say, "I really wanted to see that Indian grave."

"Yes," he says, "yes . . . so did I."

I turn and walk east, away from the windmill. I watch the next swell of prairie in front of me. I walk until I am on top of the swell, and then I stop. You can see both ways here. I stay there only a moment; then I continue east knowing that over the next swell will be the Indian grave.

[1988]

1. "I thank God this is not my home," the narrator says (lines 9–10) as he walks to the homestead where his grandfather had lived. Why does the narrator feel that way? Why does he think of the windmill as a "lighthouse" (line 44)?

2. What picture of the grandfather do we get from the narrator's memories (lines 20–33, 64–66, 138–144, and 219–23) of the one week they spent together? Why do you suppose the grandfather had never visited with his grandson before?

3. The narrator's only other visit to the homestead had been forty years earlier, on the day of his grandfather's funeral.

   a. Why do you think the narrator's father wanted to visit the homestead that day?

   b. Why were the black cowboy boots "exactly the kind" (line 49) that the five-year-old boy wanted? Where had he seen boots like that before? Why was the boy excited about seeing his grandfather's homestead?

   c. Why did the boy start to lose interest (lines 84–86)? How did the father restore the boy's enthusiasm (lines 88–117)?

4. When the father and son reached the windmill, the father became lost in thought. Describing the scene, the narrator, in the boy's voice, says, "I . . . try to make myself thinner because I don't want to get in the way" (lines 217–18). Get in the way of what? What does the narrator imagine his father was thinking about?

5. What does the narrator mean by saying (lines 236–37) that finally the new boots hurt so much that "no wagon full of settlers [could] stop the tears"? Why had the boy's tears dried before they even got back to the car? Why did receiving a pocketknife make the boy "feel older" (line

259)? Why do you think that the father also looked older at that moment?

6. What can the reader infer—understand from what is suggested, rather than stated directly—from the following statements?

   a. This day, though, calls for silence. (lines 123–24)

   b. . . . I can feel Father's strong hands, and as I hold the knife now I do not want to let go. (lines 130–31)

   c. I am certain because I know what it is like to lose your father. (lines 134–35)

7. After wishing that someone would "fill this place [the homestead] with laughter" (line 136), the adult narrator suddenly remembers a time that he had filled a place with laughter that he didn't understand. Why did the adults laugh when the boy asked his grandfather, "How long were you in jail?" (line 138)

8. The grandfather's story about the windmill begins in lines 67–79 and is completed in lines 145–207. What elements of the story seem probable? Which elements are possible? Which elements are impossible, making it a "tall tale"?

9. The father says to the narrator (lines 95–99), "There's nothing out here to look at to see if you're going in a straight line. . . . You get down in between two swells and *you can't see where you're going or where you've been.* The only thing that keeps you going is hope and that next swell . . . ." [Emphasis added.] How could that description of the landscape be a metaphor (a way of explaining one thing in terms of something else) for the narrator's life and perhaps the lives of his father and grandfather?

Developing a Way with Words

1. How does the figurative language (printed in dark type) in the following sentences create a picture of the land where the story is set? How does each simile (a direct

comparison) and metaphor (an implied comparison) in the following sentences suggest the general starkness of the setting—the nearly total absence of any distinctive sound or feature?

a. All sounds are **sifted** here, **broken up** by the prairie, **digested** and **dispersed in fine pieces** through the air. (lines 2–3)

b. [The sky] is **a solid blue sheet** meeting brown prairie in one straight line **as if someone had pasted two pieces of colored paper together.** (lines 6–8)

c. [The town of Arickeree, with elm trees lining each of its five paved streets,] looks **like an oasis** as you approach it from the state highway . . . . (lines 13–15)

d. When I walk I feel **as if I am climbing over ocean waves.** I am **surrounded by waves,** and though **the waves don't move,** I still feel threatened. (lines 39–42)

e. There was the windmill, just above the horizon, **pushing up** higher and higher over the next swell with each step **as if it were growing out of the prairie.** (lines 119–21)

2. The narrator's stark description of the landscape contrasts with the grandfather's colorful telling of his tall tale. In the following sentences, find an example of each of three figures of speech: simile, allusion (an indirect reference to a person or event that the reader is expected to recognize), and personification (talking about something that isn't alive as though it could think and feel). Then discuss what each figure of speech means.

a. There was never a time when it had rained for twelve days on the prairie. It was as if the ground didn't know what to do with all that water, so for a while the water just stayed there, ... (lines 149–52)

b. Before Grandfather could do anything, though, Scooter was off and running on top of the water just like Jesus Christ. (lines 189–90)

c. Grandfather's brain was swiveling around faster than a weather cock in a tornado, ... (lines 197–98)

Making Connections

1. Why do you think the author braided together the four stories—the grandfather's story about the windmill, the week his grandfather spent with them, the day he went to the homestead with his father, and the day when he is telling the story—rather than presenting them individually in chronological order? What ways of establishing connections between generations do the stories show?

2. What does the Indian grave represent, first to the narrator's father and then to the narrator himself? What connection can you see between the two walks to the grave and the title of the story?

3. Have you ever been in a position, literally or figuratively, where you couldn't see where you had been or where you were going? If so, was it a case, as in the father's analysis, of being able to keep going only because of hope?

4. If you knew one or more of your grandparents when you were a child, can you remember a specific incident involving you and one of them? Did any of your grandparents tell you stories? If so, can you remember and retell one of the stories?

5. What stereotype of American Indians does the grandfather's tall tale make use of? How does that stereotype compare with the picture presented in Leslie Marmon Silko's "The Man to Send Rain Clouds"?

6. In this story, as in "Secrets" by Judy Troy and "The Sojourner" by Carson McCullers, a father has died. In this story, as in "The Somebody" by Danny Santiago and "English as a Second Language" by Lucy Honig, there are tensions between a parent and child. For a paper, choose one of those four stories to compare and contrast with "Where You Have Been, Where You Are Going." Focus on the effect of a father's death on the main character in the story, or on the parent-child relationships in each of the two stories, or on another common point that interests you.

Christmas Snow

"First, standing in the doorway but still outside, he stripped three gloves from each hand and tossed them ahead of him into the shed."

Christmas Snow

Donald Hall
(born 1928)

Since his undergraduate days at Harvard, Donald Hall, the Poet Laureate of the state of New Hampshire, has been a prolific writer, publishing poetry, prose, short stories, and children's stories at the rate of four books a year. Hall's interest in writing began at the age of seven, he has said, when he was home for several weeks with a childhood illness. Bored with fifteen-minute serials on the radio, he turned to a school storybook. "Thus I became fluent with reading for the first time," Hall recounts, "and discovered the bliss of abandonment to print, to word and story. From the love of reading [came] the desire to write, a lifelong commitment to making things that might (if I were diligent, talented, and lucky) resemble the books I loved reading."*

Grace in expressing his ideas and a generous enthusiasm for the work of others are two of Hall's distinguishing characteristics. In *Remembering Poets* (1977; revised and republished as *Their Ancient Glittering Eyes,* 1992), Hall combined mature literary criticism with anecdotes of his youthful meetings with four of the twentieth century's major poets: Dylan Thomas, Robert Frost, T. S. Eliot, and Ezra Pound. His collected short stories, published as *The Ideal Bakery* (1987), is dedicated to his fellow poets Raymond Carver (represented in volume 1 of this text) and Tess Gallagher. In *Life Work* (1993), Hall speaks of the importance of work in his life and that of his forebearers, including the people who appear in "Christmas Snow." His earlier

---

* From Donald Hall, "The Books Not Read, the Lines Not Written: A Poet Confronts His Mortality." *The New York Times Book Review,* August 1, 1993.

autobiographical memoir *String Too Short To Be Saved* (1961) tells of the same New Hampshire family.

In "Christmas Snow," a middle-aged narrator, Donnie, remembers "the snows of Christmas in New Hampshire" in 1938, the year of his tenth birthday. The story is framed, like a picture, by events from the evening of December 23 to the evening of December 24; other events, both recent and distant, are presented within the frame. During the day, three generations of family members talk of their experience with heavy snow in other years. By the time Donnie has been sent to bed, long past his usual bedtime, his knowledge of the world has, in the words of the poet Yeats, been changed utterly.

When *The Ideal Bakery* appeared in 1987, novelist and short-story writer John Casey called the book "brilliant" and "a flare of beauty and pity." Singling out "Christmas Snow" for special praise, the reviewer confessed that rereading the story before writing his review, he "was startled to tears all over again the second time through." How could a story cause a man to cry both the first and second times he reads it? And how could it take him by surprise the second time? What will change Donnie's view of the world? To find out for yourself, read on.

Uncommon Words or Meanings

a hurricane ("too busy looking for *hurricane* damage")—a storm with violent winds of more than seventy–five miles an hour; it may be combined with a **cyclone,** a strong wind rotating around a calm central area. The grandfather in this story jokes about "Harry Cane" and "Si Clone."

to corduroy ("logs . . . that would *corduroy* the surface of . . . lakes for years.")—create a surface with parallel ridges, like those in the cotton fabric called corduroy.

chains ("chewed the rest with *chains*")—links of heavy metal put around automobile tires to keep them from spinning on snow or ice.

to pack ("to see if it would *pack*")—to become a firm mass when pressed together.

a hoptoad ("Fred wasn't much bigger than a *hoptoad*")—a small amphibious animal, similar to a frog.

Vicksburg ("fought at *Vicksburg*")—a city in Mississippi, the site of a decisive Northern victory in April 1863 in the American Civil War.

Kathleen Norris ("a novel by *Kathleen Norris*")—a popular American writer of the day, the author of more than eighty romantic novels and many short stories.

the Hardy Boys ("a *Hardy Boys* mystery")—a popular series of adventure books for boys.

a toadstool ("the dark *toadstool* of the birdbath")—a poisonous mushroom.

to farm out ("his family had . . . *farmed* him *out* to the Keneston cousins")—to let (something) be used temporarily in exchange for payment; here, send a child to live with relatives because his own family couldn't afford to feed and clothe him.

a plow ("I suppose Benjamin's *plow* broke down again.")—a snowplow, a machine for moving large quantities of snow to clear a road.

leastways ("*Leastways,* we're all here for the night.")—(informal) anyway, in any case.

John Greenleaf Whittier ("It's *John Greenleaf Whittier,* 'Snowbound'")—a nineteenth-century American poet whose poem "Snowbound," first published in 1866, was a standard of elementary school English classes for close to one hundred years.

grace ("Uncle Luther said *grace.*")—a short prayer of thanks said before eating.

Zane Grey ("new *Zane Grey* books")—the author of many popular Westerns, including *Riders of the Purple Sage.*

a scholar ("Nannie wouldn't let her *scholars* go home")—(through the nineteenth century) a child being taught in a school.

a town meeting ("Christmas and *town meeting*")—In New England, a meeting of the qualified voters of a town to discuss and act on public business.

a stone wall ("walked back to town on the tops of *stone walls*")—a low wall (perhaps three feet high and a foot wide), made by laying stones one on top of another, common in New England.

Christmas Snow

The real snows I remember are the snows of Christmas in New Hampshire. I was ten years old, and there was a night when I woke up to the sound of grown-ups talking. Slowly, I realized that it wasn't that at all; the mounds of my grandfather and
5 grandmother lay still in their bed under many quilts in the cold room. It was rain falling and rubbing against the bushes outside my windows. I sat up in bed, pulling the covers around me, and held the green shade out from the frosty pane. There were flakes of snow mixed into the rain—large, slow flakes fluttering down
10 like wet leaves. I watched as long as I could, until the back of my neck hurt with the cold, while the flakes grew thicker and the snow took over the rain. When I looked up into the dark sky, just before lying back in my warm feather bed, the whole air was made of fine light shapes. I was happy in my own world of snow,
15 as if I were living inside one of those glass paperweights that snow when you shake them, and I went back to sleep easily. In the morning, I looked out the window as soon as I woke. There were no more leaves, no more weeds turned brown by the frost, no sheds, no road, and no chicken coops. The sky was a dense
20 mass of snowflakes, the ground covered in soft white curves.

It was the morning of Christmas Eve, 1938. The day before, we had driven north from Connecticut, and I had been disappointed to find that there was no snow on my grandfather's farm. On the trip up, I had not noticed the lack of snow
25 because I was too busy looking for hurricane damage. (September 1938 was the time of the great New England hurricane.) Maples and oaks and elms were down everywhere. Huge roots stood up like dirt cliffs next to the road. On distant hillsides, whole stands of trees lay pointing in the same direc-
30 tion, like combed hair. Men were cutting the timber with double handsaws, their breaths blue-white in the cold. Ponds were already filling with logs—stored timber that would corduroy the surface of New Hampshire lakes for years. Here and there I saw a roof gone from a barn, or a tree leaning into a house.

35 We knew from letters that my grandfather's farmhouse was all right. I was excited to be going there, sitting in the front seat between my mother and father, with the heater blasting at my knees. Every summer we drove the same route and I spent two weeks following my grandfather as he did chores, listen-

40 ing to his talk. The familiar road took shape again: Sunapee, Georges Mills, New London; then there was the shortcut along the bumpy Cilleyville Road. We drove past the West Andover depot, past Henry's store and the big rock, and climbed the lit-tle hill by the Blasington's, and there, down the slope to the

45 right, we saw the lights of the farmhouse. In a porch window I could see my small Christmas tree, with its own string of lights. It stood in the window next to the large one, where I could see it when we drove over the hill.

We stopped in the driveway and the kitchen door loosened

50 a wedge of yellow light. My grandfather stood in his milking clothes, tall and bald and smiling broadly. He lifted me up, grunting at how big I was getting. Over his shoulder, which smelled happily of barn and tie-up, I saw my grandmother in her best dress, waiting her turn and looking pleased.

55 As we stood outside in the cold, I looked around for the signs of the hurricane. In the light from the kitchen window I could just see a stake with a rope tied to it that angled up into the tall maple by the shed. Then I remembered that my grand-mother had written my mother about that tree. It had blown

60 over, roots out of the ground, and Washington Woodward, a cousin of ours who lived on Ragged Mountain, was fixing it. The great tree was upright now.

My grandfather saw me looking at it. "Looks like it's going to work, don't it? Of course you can't tell until spring, and the

65 leaves. A lot of the root must have gone." He shook his head. "Wash is a wonder," he said. "He winched that tree back upright in two days with a pulley on that oak." He pointed to a tree on the hill in back of the house. "I thought he was going to pull that oak clear out of the ground. Then he took that rock-

70 moving machine of his" (I remembered that Wash had con-structed a wooden tripod about fifteen feet high for moving rocks. I never understood how it worked, though I heard him explain it a hundred times. He moved rocks for fun mostly; it was his hobby.) "and moved that boulder down from the pas-

75 ture and set it there to keep the roots flat. It only took him five days in all, and I think he saved the tree."

It was when we moved back to the group around the car that I realized, with sudden disappointment, that there was no snow on the ground.

* * *

I turned from the window the next morning and looked over at my grandparents' bed. My grandmother was there, but the place beside her was empty. The clock on the bureau, among snapshots and perfume bottles, said six o'clock. I heard my grandfather carrying wood into the living room. Logs crashed into the big, square stove. In a moment I heard another sound I had been listening for—a massive animal roar from the same stove. He had poured a tin can of kerosene on the old embers and the new logs. Then I heard him fix the kitchen stove and pause by the door to put on coats and scarves and a cap—his boots were in the shed—and then the door shut between the kitchen and the shed, and he had gone to milk the cows.

It was warm inside my bed. My grandmother stood up beside her bed, her gray hair down to her waist. "Good morning," she said. "You awake? We've had some snow. You go back to sleep while I make the doughnuts." That brought me out of bed quickly. I dressed next to the stove in the dark living room. The sides of the stove glowed red, and I kept my distance. The cold of the room almost visibly receded into the farther corners, there to dwindle into something the size of a pea.

My grandmother was fixing her hair in the warm kitchen, braiding it and winding it up on her head. She looked like my grandmother again. "Doughnuts won't be ready for a long time. Fat's got to heat. Why don't you have a slice of bread and go see Gramp in the tie-up?"

I put peanut butter on the bread and bundled up with galoshes and a wool cap that I could pull over my ears. I stepped outside into the swirl of flakes, white against the gray of the early morning. It was my first snow of the year, and it set my heart pounding with pleasure. But even if it had snowed in Connecticut earlier, this would have been my first real snow. When it snowed in Connecticut, the snowplows heaped most of it in the gutters and the cars chewed the rest with chains and blackened it with oil. Here the snow turned the farm into a planet of its own, an undiscovered moon.

I walked past our Studebaker, which was humped already with two inches of snow. I reached down for a handful, to see if it would pack, but it was dry as cotton. The flakes, when I looked up into the endless flaking barrel of the sky, were fine

120 and constant. It was going to snow all day. I climbed the hill to the barn without lifting my galoshes quite clear of the snow and left two long trenches behind me. I raised the iron latch and went into the tie-up, shaking my head and shoulders like a dog, making a little snowstorm inside.

125 My grandfather laughed. "It's really coming down," he said. "It'll be a white Christmas, you can be sure of that."

"I love it," I said.

"Can you make a snowman today?"

"It's dry snow," I said. "It won't pack."

130 "When it melts a little, you can roll away the top of it—I mean, tomorrow or the next day. I remember making a big one with my brother Fred when I was nine—no, eight. Fred wasn't much bigger than a hoptoad then. I called him Hoptoad when I wanted to make him mad, and my, you never saw such a red

135 face. Well, we spent the whole day Saturday making this great creature. Borrowed a scarf and an old hat—it was a woman's hat, but we didn't mind—and a carrot from the cellar for the nose, and two little potatoes for the eyes. It was a fine thing, no doubt about it, and we showed your Aunt Lottie, who said

140 it was the best one she ever saw. Then my father came out of the forge—putting things away for the Sabbath, you know, shutting things away—and he saw what we'd been up to and came over and stood in front of it. I can see him now, so tall, with his big brown beard. We were proud of that snowman,

145 and I guess we were waiting for praise. 'Very good, boys,' he said." Here my grandfather's voice turned deep and impressive. "'That's a fine snowman. It's too bad you put him in front of the shed. You can take him down now.'" My grandfather laughed. "Of course, we felt bad, but we felt silly, too. The back

150 of that snowman was almost touching the carriage we drove to church in. We were tired with making it, and I guess we were tired when we came in for supper! I suppose that was the last snowman I ever made."

I loved him to tell his stories. His voice filled the white-

155 washed, cobwebby tie-up. I loved his imitations, and the glimpses of an old time. In this story I thought my great-grand-father sounded cruel; there must have some *other* way to get to church. But I didn't really care. I never really got upset by my grandfather's stories, no matter what happened in them. All

the characters were fabulous, and none more so than his strong blacksmith father, who had fought at Vicksburg.

My grandfather was milking now, not heavily dressed against the cold but most of the time wedged between the bodies of two huge holsteins, which must have given off a good bit of heat. The alternate streams of milk went swush-swush from his fists into the pail, first making a tinny sound and then softening and becoming more liquid as the pail filled. When he wasn't speaking, he leaned his head on the rib cage of a cow, the visor of his cap turned around to the back like a baseball catcher's. When he spoke, he tilted his head back and turned toward me. He sat on an old easy chair with the legs cut off, while I had taken down a three-legged stool from a peg on the wall. We talked about the hurricane a bit, and he made jokes about "Harry Cane" and "Si Clone." Whenever the pail was full, he would take it to the milk room and strain it into the big milk can, which the truck would pick up later in the day. We went from cow to cow, from Sally to Spot to Betty to Alice Weaver. And then we were done. While the last milk strained into the big can, I helped my grandfather clean out the tie-up, hoeing the cowflops through the floor onto the manure heap under the barn. Then he fitted tops on the milk cans and craned them onto his wheelbarrow. I unlatched the door and we went into the snow.

The trenches that I had scraped with my galoshes were filled in. The boulder that Washington Woodward had rolled over the roots of the maple wore a thick white cap; it looked like an enormous snowball. The air was a chaff of white motes, the tiny dry flakes. (I remembered last summer in the barn, sneezing with the fine dust while my grandfather pitched hay.) The iron wheel of the wheelbarrow made a narrow cut in the snow and spun a long delicate arc of snow forward. Our four boots made a new trail. Crossing the road to the platform on the other side, we hardly knew where the road began and the ditch ended. We were all alone with no trace of anything else in the world. We came back to the kitchen for breakfast, slapping our hands and stamping our feet, exhilarated with cold and with the first snow of winter.

I smelled the doughnuts when we opened the door from the shed to the kitchen. My father was standing in the kitchen,

200 wearing a light sweater over an open-neck shirt, smoking his before-breakfast cigarette. On the stove, the fat was bubbling, and I could see the circles of dough floating and turning brown. When she saw me, my grandmother tossed a few more dough-nuts into the fat, and I watched them greedily as they floated
205 among the bubbles. In a moment, my mother came downstairs, and we all ate doughnuts and drank milk and coffee.

"Is it going to snow all day?" my father asked my grandfather.

"It looks so," said my grandfather.

"I hope the girls can get through," said my grandmother.
210 She always worried about things. My mother's schoolteacher sisters were expected that night.

"They will, Katie," said my grandfather.

"They have chains, I suppose," said my father.

"Oh, yes," said my grandfather, "and they're good drivers."
215 "Who else is coming?" I asked.

"Uncle Luther," said my grandfather, "and Wash. Wash will have to find his way down Ragged."

That morning after breakfast, my Aunt Caroline arrived, and before noon my Aunt Nan. Each of them talked with me
220 for a while, and then each of them was absorbed by the kitchen and preparations for tomorrow's dinner. I kept looking at the presents under both trees—a pile for the grown-ups under the branches of the big tree, and almost as many under mine. After lunch, Nan drove up to "Sabine," Uncle Luther's
225 small house a quarter mile north, and brought him back. He was my grandmother's older brother, a clergyman who had retired from his city parish and was preaching at the little South Danbury church that we went to in New Hampshire. My grandfather disappeared for a while—nobody would tell me
230 where he was—and a little later my grandmother was plucking feathers from a hen named Old Rusty that had stopped laying eggs. Then my grandfather dressed up in a brown suit, because it was Christmas Eve, and read a novel by Kathleen Norris. My father read magazines or paced up and down with a cigarette.
235 I must have seemed restless, because after a while my father plucked one of my presents from under my tree and told me to open it. It was a Hardy Boys mystery. I sat in the living room with my father and grandfather and read a Christmas book.

By four-thirty, it was a perfectly dark, and the snow kept
240 coming. When I looked out in the sitting-room window, past

the light the windows cast into the front yard, I saw darkness with shadows of snow upon it. Inside the cup of light, the snow floated like feathers. It piled high on the little round stones on each side of the path from the driveway. Farther on in the darkness I could see the dark toadstool of the birdbath weighted down under an enormous puff of whiteness. I went to the kitchen window to look at our car, but there was only a car-shaped drift of snow, with indentations for the windows.

245

It was time for milking again. My grandfather bundled up with extra socks and sweaters and scarves, and long boots over his suit trousers, and my grandmother pinned his coat around his neck with a huge safety pin. She always fretted about his health. She had also been fretting for an hour over Washington Woodward. (Wash had been sort of an older brother to her when she was a little girl; his family had been poor and had farmed him out to the Keneston cousins.) My grandfather stepped out the shed door and sank into the snow. He started to take big steps toward the barn when suddenly he stopped and we heard him shout, "Katie, Donnie, look!" Peering out the shed window, we could just see my grandfather in the reflected light from the kitchen. He was pointing past that light, and while we watched, a figure moved into it, pacing slowly with a shuffling sort of gait. Then the figure said, "Wesley!" and started talking, and we knew it was Wash.

250

255

260

It would have been hard to tell what it was if it hadn't talked. Wash looked as if he was wearing six coats, and the outermost was the pelt of a deer. He shot one every winter and dried its pelt on the side of his hut; I think the pelts served to keep out the wind, for one thing. His face was almost covered with horizontal strips of brown cloth, covered with snow now, leaving just a slit for the eyes. The same sort of strips, arranged vertically, fastened his cap to his head and tied under his chin.

265

270

When he shuffled up to the shed door, my grandmother opened it. "Snowshoes," she said. "I knew that's how you'd do it, maybe." She laughed—with relief I suppose, and also at Wash's appearance. Wash was talking—he was always talking— but I didn't notice what he said. I was too busy watching him take off his snowshoeing clothes. First, standing in the doorway but still outside, he stripped three gloves from each hand and tossed them ahead of him into the shed. It was even cold for us to stand watching him in the open door, but Wash had to take

275

280

off his snowshoes before he could come inside. His thick cold fingers fumbled among leather thongs. Finally, he stood out of them, and stepped inside. As we closed the shed door, I saw my grandfather trudge up the blue hill toward the barn.

285

A single naked light bulb burned at the roof of the shed. Wash stamped his feet and found his gloves and put them on a table. All the time, his voice went on and on. "About there, McKenzie's old place, my left shoe got loose. I had to stop there by the big rock and fix it. It took me a while, because I didn't have a good place to put my foot. Well, I was standing there pretty quiet, getting my breath, when a red fox came sniffing along. . . ."

290

Now he began taking off the layers of his clothing. He unknotted the brown bands around his face, and they turned into long socks. "How do you like these, Katie?" he interrupted himself. "You gave them to me last Christmas, and I hain't worn them yet." He went on with his story. When all the socks were peeled off, they revealed his beard. Beards were rare in 1938. I saw a few in New Hampshire, usually on old men. Washington shaved his beard every spring and grew it again in the fall, so I knew two Washington Woodwards—the summer one and the winter one. The beard was brown-gray, and it served him most of the winter instead of a scarf. It was quite full already and wagged as he talked. His eyes crinkled in the space left between the two masses of his beard and his hair. Wash never cut his hair in winter, either—also for the sake of warmth. He thought we should use the hair God gave us before we went to adding other things.

295

300

305

He unwound himself now, taking off the pelt of the deer, which was frozen and stiff, and then a series of coats and jackets. Then there was a pair of overalls, then I saw that he had wrapped burlap bags around his shins and thighs, underneath the legs of the overalls, and tied them in place with bits of string. It took him a long time to undo the knots, but he refused to cut them away with a knife; that would have been a waste. Then he was down to his boots, his underneath overalls, his old much-mended shirt, and a frail brown cardigan over it. He took off his boots, and we walked through the kitchen and into the living room.

310

315

Everyone welcomed Wash, and we heard him tell about his four-hour walk down Ragged on snowshoes, about the red fox and the car he saw abandoned. "Come to think of it," my father said, "I haven't heard any traffic going past."

320

Wash interrupted his own monologue. "Nothing can get
through just now. It's a bad storm. I suppose Benjamin's plow
broke down again. Leastways we're all here for the night."

"Snowbound," said Uncle Luther.

"Got the wood in?" Washington asked my grandfather.

Aunt Nan recited:

> Shut in from all the world without,
> We sat the clean-winged hearth about,
> Content to let the north-wind roar
> In baffled rage at pane and door,
> While the red logs before us beat
> The frost-line back with tropic heat . . .

She giggled when she was through.

Aunt Caroline said, "I remember when we had to learn that."

"Miss Headley," my mother said. She turned to me. "Do you
have that in school? It's John Greenleaf Whittier, 'Snowbound.'"

"Are we really snowbound?" I said. I liked the idea of it. I
felt cozy and protected, walled in by the snow. I wanted it to
keep on snowing all winter, so that I wouldn't have to back to
Connecticut and school.

"If we have to get out, we'll get out," my father said quickly.

In a moment, my grandfather came in from milking, his
cheeks red from the cold. My grandmother and her daughters
went out to the kitchen, and the men added leaves to the dining-room table. We sat down to eat, and Uncle Luther said
grace. On the table, the dishes were piled high with boiled
potatoes and carrots and string beans, boiled beef, and white
bread. Everyone passed plates to and fro and talked all at
once. My two aunts vied over me, teasing and praising.

"How was the hurricane up your way?" I heard my father
say to Wash. He had to interrupt Wash to say it, but it was the
only way you could ever ask Wash a question.

As I'm sure my father expected, it got Wash started. "I was
coming back from chasing some bees—I found a hive, all right,
but I needed a ladder—and I saw the sky looking mighty peculiar
down South Pasture way, and . . ." He told every motion he made
and named every tree that fell on his land and the land of his
neighbors. When he spoke about it, the hurricane took on a sort
of malevolent personality, like someone cruel without reason.

The rest of the table talked hurricane, too. My grandfather
told about a rowboat that somehow moved half a mile from

its pond. My aunts talked about their towns, my father of
how the tidal wave had wrecked his brother's island off the
Connecticut coast. I told about walking home from school
with a model airplane in my hand and how a gust of wind took
370   it out of my hand and whirled it away and I never found it. (I
didn't say that my father bought me another one the next day.)
I had the sudden vision of all of us—the whole family, from
Connecticut to New Hampshire—caught in the same storm.
Suppose a huge wind had picked us up in its fists? . . . We
375   might have met over Massachusetts.

After supper, we moved to the living room. In our family,
the grown-ups had their presents on Christmas Eve and the
children had Christmas morning all to themselves. (In 1938 I
was the only child there was.) I was excited. The fire in the
380   open stove burned hot, the draft ajar at the bottom and the flue
open in the chimney. We heard the wind blowing outside in the
darkness and saw white flakes of snow hurtle against the
black windowpanes. We were warm.
I distributed the presents, reading the names on the tags
385   and trying to keep them flowing evenly. Drifts of wrapping
paper rose beside each chair, and on laps there were new Zane
Grey books, toilet water, brown socks and work shirts, bars of
soap, and bracelets and neckties. Sentences of package opening ("Now *what* could *this* be?") gave way to sentences of
390   appreciation ("I certainly can use some handkerchiefs, Caroline!"). The bright packages were combed from the branches
of the big tree, and the floor was bare underneath. My eyes
kept moving toward a pile under and around the small tree.
"Do you remember the oranges, Katie?" said Uncle Luther.
395   My grandmother nodded. "Didn't they taste good!" she
said. She giggled. "I can't think they taste like that anymore."
My grandfather said, "Christmas and town meeting, that's
when we had them. The man came to town meeting and sold
them there, too." He was talking to me. "They didn't have
400   oranges much in those days," he said. "They were a great treat
for the children at Christmas."
"Oranges and popcorn balls," said my grandmother.
"And clothes," said Uncle Luther. "Mittens and warm clothes."
My grandfather went out into the kitchen, and we heard him
405   open the door. When we came back, he said, "It's snowing and
blowing still. I reckon it's a blizzard, all right. It's starting to drift."

"It won't be like '88," Uncle Luther. "It's too early in the year."

"What month was the blizzard of '88?" said my father.

Uncle Luther, my grandfather, and my grandmother all started to talk at once. Then my grandparents laughed and deferred to Uncle Luther. "March 11 to 14," he said. "I guess Nannie, would have remembered, all right." My great-aunt Nannie, who had died earlier that year, was a sister of Uncle Luther and my grandmother.

"Why?" said my father.

"She was teaching school, a little school back of Grafton, in the hills. She used to tell this story every time it started to snow, and we teased her for saying it so much. It snowed so hard and drifted so deep Nannie wouldn't let her scholars go home. All of them, and Nannie, too, had to spend the night. They ran out of wood for the stove, and she wouldn't let anyone go outside to get some more wood—she was afraid he'd get lost in the snow and the dark—so they broke up three desks, the old-fashioned kind they used to have in those old schoolhouses. She said those boys really loved to break up those desks and see them burn. In the morning, some of the farmers came and got them out."

For a moment, everyone was quiet—I suppose, thinking of Nannie. Then my father—my young father, who is dead now—spoke up: "My father likes to tell about the blizzard of '88, too. They have a club down in Connecticut that meets once a year and swaps stories about it. He was a boy on the farm out in Hamden, and they drove the sleigh all the way into New Haven the next day. The whole country was nothing but snow. They never knew whether they were on a road or not. They went right across Lake Whitney, on top of fences and all. It took them eight hours to go four miles."

"We just used to call it the big snow," said my grandmother. "Papa was down in Danbury for town meeting. Everybody was gone away from home overnight, because it was town meeting everyplace. Then in the morning he came back on a wild engine."

I looked at my grandfather.

"An engine that's loose—that's not pulling anything," he explained.

"It stopped to let him off right down there," my grandmother continued. She pointed through the parlor, toward the front door and across the road and past the chickens and sheep, to the railroad track a hundred yards away. "In back of

the sheep barn. Just for him. We were excited about him riding
the wild engine."

"My father had been to town meeting, too," said my grandfather. "He tried to walk home along the flats and the meadow,
but he had to turn back. When it was done, my brothers and I
walked to town on the tops of stone walls. You couldn't see the
stones, but you could tell from how the snow lay." Suddenly I
could see the three young men, my grandfather in the lead, single-filing through the snow, bundled up and their arms outstretched, balancing like tightrope walkers.

Washington spoke, and made it obvious that he had been
listening. He had broken his monologue to hear. "I remember
that snow," he said.

I settled down for the interminable story. It was late and I
was sleepy. I knew that soon the grown-ups would notice me
and pack me off to bed.

"I remember it because it was the worst day of my life,"
said Wash.

"What?" said my father. He only spoke in surprise. No one
expected anything from Wash but harangues of process—how
I moved the rock, how I shot the bear, how I snowshoed down
Ragged.

"It was my father," said Wash. "He hated me." (Then I
remembered, dimly, hearing that Wash's father was a cruel
man. The world of cruel fathers was as far from me as the
world of stepmothers who fed poisoned apples to stepdaughters.) "He hated me from the day I was born."

"He wasn't a good man, Wash," said my grandmother. She
always understated everything, but this time I saw her eyes
flick over at me, and I realized she was afraid for me. Then I
looked around the room and saw all eyes except Washington's
were glancing at me.

"That Christmas, '87," Washington said, "the Kenestons'
folks" (he meant my grandmother's family) "gave me skates.
I'd never had any before. And they were the good, new, steel
kind, not the old iron ones where you had to have an iron plate
fixed to your shoe. There were screws on these, and you just
clamped them to your shoes. I was fifteen years old."

"I remember," said Uncle Luther. "They were my skates,
and then I broke my kneecap and I couldn't skate anymore. I
can almost remember the name."

490 "Peck & Snider," said Wash. "They were Peck & Snider skates. I skated whenever I didn't have chores. That March tenth I skated for maybe I thought the last time that year, and I hung them on a nail over my bed in the loft when I got home. I was skating late, by the moon, after chores. My legs were good

495 then. In the morning, I slept late—I was tired—and my father took my skates away because I was late for chores. That was the day it started to snow."

"What a terrible thing to do," said my grandfather.

"He took them out to the pond where I skated," said Wash,

500 "and he made me watch. He cut a hole in the ice with his hatchet. It was snowing already. I begged him not to, but he dropped those Peck & Snider skates into the water, right down out of sight into Eagle Pond."

Uncle Luther shook his head. No one said anything. My

505 father looked at the floor.

Washington was staring straight ahead, fifteen years old again and full of hatred. I could see his mouth moving inside the gray-brown beard. "We stayed inside for four days. Couldn't open a door for the snow. I always hated the snow. I had to

510 keep looking at him."

After a minute when no one spoke, Aunt Caroline turned to me and made silly guesses about the presents under my tree. I recognized diversionary tactics. Other voices took up several conversations around the room. Then my mother leapt upon

515 me, saying it was *two hours* past my bedtime, and in five minutes I was warming my feather bed, hearing the grown-up voices dim and far away like wind, like the wind and snow outside my window.

[1987]

Understanding the Story

1. Where is Donnie as the story begins and ends? What sound does he hear on both occasions?

2. On the day of December 23, what had occupied Donnie's attention on the drive (probably a four- or five-hour trip) from Connecticut to New Hampshire?

3. What caused Donnie to feel "sudden disappointment" (line 78) as he looked around the farm? The next morning, December 24, when he went outdoors before breakfast, what "set [his] heart pounding with pleasure" (lines 109–10)?

4. When Donnie complained that the snow was too dry to make a snowman, his grandfather told him (lines 131–53) about making a snowman in his own childhood.

   a. What was special about the snowman that the grandfather and his brother made?

   b. What act in the story made Donnie think of his great-grandfather as "cruel" (line 157)? What other act of paternal cruelty does this foreshadow (give the reader a hint of)?

   c. Why do you suppose the grandfather, after more than fifty years, still remembered that event so clearly?

5. Looking at the family tree on the facing page, find the five people who were already in the house on the morning of December 24. Then find the other four who were expected during the day. Then make up a question about the family tree to ask your classmates. For example, how old were "the girls" (line 209) whose safety the grandmother was worried about? (Except for the names and dates in square brackets, which are drawn from Hall's *Life Work,* all of the information on the family tree appears in "Christmas Snow.")

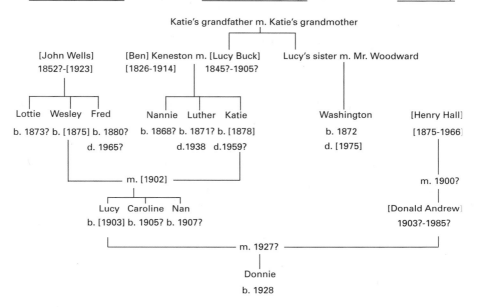

Grandfather's Family | Grandmother's Family | [Hall] Family

Katie's grandfather m. Katie's grandmother

[John Wells] 1852?-[1923]

[Ben] Keneston m. [Lucy Buck] [1826-1914] 1845?-1905?

Lucy's sister m. Mr. Woodward

Lottie b. 1873? | Wesley b. [1875] | Fred b. 1880? d. 1965?

Nannie b. 1868? | Luther b. 1871? d.1938 | Katie b. [1878] d.1959?

Washington b. 1872 d. [1975]

[Henry Hall] [1875-1966]

m. [1902]

Lucy b. [1903] | Caroline b. 1905? | Nan b. 1907?

m. 1900?

[Donald Andrew] 1903?-1985?

m. 1927?

Donnie b. 1928

6. On Christmas Eve afternoon, what was Donnie's grandfather doing when he "disappeared for a while" (line 229)? In the "preparations for tomorrow's dinner" (line 221), what task did Donnie's grandmother have? What details suggest how Donnie's grandfather, father, and Donnie himself felt about spending most of the afternoon sitting still?

7. Late in the afternoon, a "figure" (line 262) appeared out of the dark. What explains the narrator's assertion, "It would have been hard to tell what it [the figure] was if it hadn't talked" (lines 265–66)? Who was the strangely-dressed figure? Why had he taken a "four-hour walk down Ragged [Mountain] on snowshoes" (line 321) rather than coming by car, as everyone else had?

8. The story is studded with references to the "great New England hurricane" (lines 26–27) of the previous September. For example, the grandfather reported how Washington Woodward had saved a large uprooted tree (lines 66–76), and Donnie's grandfather joked about

"Harry Cane" and "Si Clone" (line 174). Over the Christmas Eve supper, everyone was still talking about the storm.

a. The narrator observes that when Wash talked of the hurricane, it "took on a sort of malevolent personality, like someone cruel without reason" (lines 362–63). How does this foreshadow the story that Wash later tells about his father?

b. What was Donnie's hurricane story? What part did he leave out? Why?

9. Americans who celebrate Christmas usually open their presents on Christmas morning. Why, in Donnie's family, did the grown-ups open their presents on Christmas Eve? What ritual present-opening phrases did they use? What do the kinds of gifts they exchanged tell you about their lives?

10. The story-telling after the presents was about "the blizzard of '88" (line 408).

a. Why do you suppose the first story was about Nannie? What happened when she was snowbound with her pupils in the winter of 1888?

b. What stories from the blizzard of '88 did the narrator's father, grandmother, and grandfather each tell about their fathers? What tone do all these stories share?

c. How was Wash's blizzard story different from the style of his earlier conversation, as well as from the other blizzard stories? What had made the day of the blizzard "the worst day of [his] life" (line 465)? Why do you think Wash's father reacted so strongly to the boy being late with his chores? What could explain why his father "hated [him] from the day [he] was born" (line 475)?

d. What details show that the other adults knew what was coming in Wash's story and did not want Donnie to hear it? Why do you think they let Wash tell the story anyway? What explains the silence when Wash stopped talking? What does the narrator mean by saying (lines 512–13), "I recognized diversionary tactics"?

11. How was the meaning of "Christmas snow" different for Donnie and Wash? (This could be a topic for writing.)

Developing a Way with Words

1. An allusion is an indirect reference, one that the author expects the reader to understand without explanation. There are two allusions in the story that you probably recognized:

   a. When the narrator speaks (lines 474–75) of "the world of stepmothers who fed poisoned apples to stepdaughters," what fairy tale is he alluding to?

   b. What well-known historical figure was Wash named for? And what is the irony (the difference between implied expectation and reality) in that choice?

2. What did Wesley mean by saying (lines 132–33) "Fred wasn't much bigger than a hoptoad then"?

3. How did Wash act on his belief (lines 308–09) that "we should use the hair God gave us before we went to adding other things"?

4. In the following sentences, three of the phrases in dark type are similes (direct comparisons) and two are examples of personification (talking about an inanimate object as though it were alive). Which is which? Which of the five senses—sight, hearing, touch, taste, and smell—does each of them call on?

   a. I was happy in my own world of snow, **as if I were living inside one of those glass paperweights that snow when you shake them** . . . . (lines 14–16)

   b. **The boulder** that Washington Woodward had rolled over the roots of the maple **wore a thick white cap**; it looked **like an enormous snowball.** (lines 185–87)

   c. I had a sudden vision of all of us—the whole family, from Connecticut to New Hampshire—caught in the same storm. Suppose a huge wind had **picked us up in its fists**? . . . We might have met over Massachusetts. (lines 372–75)

d. Suddenly I could see the three young men, my grandfather in the lead, single-filing through the snow, bundled up and their arms outstretched, balancing **like tightrope walkers.** (lines 455–58)

M aking Connections

1. Many details in the story, such as the small Christmas tree just for him, show that Donnie was a much-loved child. What are some of the other details? Who was the only adult who didn't make a fuss over him? Can you explain why that would have been?

2. Donnie, his father, his grandfather (Wesley), and his grandmother's cousin Wash each speak of their fathers. (*Donnie*: lines 199–201, 233–38, 370–71 and 429–30; *Donnie's father*: lines 429–37; *Wesley*: lines 140–54 and 451–55; and *Wash*: lines 471–503.) Examine the specific remarks about each father.

   a. As their sons present them, how are the four fathers alike? How are they different? For example, was the "cruelty" (in Donnie's eyes) of Wesley's father with the snowman similar to the cruelty of Wash's father with the skates?

   b. What story about your father is a good reflection of the way you see him?

3. What was the function of story-telling in the grandparents' home? Do the members of your family tell stories? If so, what kinds of stories are they? Does the story-telling in your family serve some—or all—of the same purposes as in Donnie's family?

4. The narrator describes the Christmas ritual in his grandparents' home with loving detail. One example is the big tree for the grown-ups and small tree for Donnie; also, while the women worked in the kitchen, the men sat restlessly in the parlor, and the same appreciative

remarks were made every year during the opening of presents. Describe your family's ritual for a specific holiday, providing as many details as possible about ritual food, dress, activities, and phrases.

5. Do you have specific memories of a hurricane, or a big snowfall, or another unusual natural event? How did it affect people physically? How did it affect them psychologically? Try to describe the event vividly. Use figurative language to describe its impact on the people and their surroundings.

6. In this story, as in "Where You Have Been, Where You Are Going" by Mark Steven Hess, a man remembers a contact with his grandfather in his childhood. In what other ways are the stories alike? In what ways are they different?

7. In 1993, the distinguished journalist Bill Moyers talked with Donald Hall and his wife, Jane Kenyon, about their lives and their work. He also filmed them in their home—the same house in which Donnie spent the memorable Christmas of this story—and at poetry readings they have given in their small New Hampshire town. Teachers in the U.S. can contact their local PBS station to see if the edition of "Bill Moyers' Journal" called "A Life Together" is scheduled for rebroadcast. Alternatively, a copy of the program can be purchased from PBS Home Video, 1320 Braddock Place, Alexandria, VA 22314; 1-800-828-4727.

Text Credits

"Hills Like White Elephants": Reprinted with permission of Charles Scribner's Sons, an imprint of Macmillan Publishing Company, from MEN WITHOUT WOMEN by Ernest Hemingway. Copyright © 1927 by Charles Scribner's Sons; renewal copyright 1955 © by Ernest Hemingway.

"The Man to Send Rain Clouds": Copyright © 1981 by Leslie Marmon Silko. Reprinted from STORYTELLER by Leslie Marmon Silko, published by Seaver Books. New York, New York.

"The Japanese Hamlet": From THE CHAUVINIST AND OTHER STORIES by Toshio Mori. Original copyright © *Harper's Bazaar*, October, 1951. Copyright © Renewed 1978 by Hisaye Yamamoto DeSoto.

"The Somebody": by Danny Santiago. Copyright © 1970, by Danny Santiago. First appeared in *Redbook* magazine. Reprinted by permission of Brandt & Brandt Literary Agents, Inc.

"I'm Nobody!": From THE COMPLETE POEMS OF EMILY DICKINSON, edited by Thomas H. Johnson, Copyright © 1960. Reprinted by permission of Little, Brown and Company.

"The Rebel": I AM A BLACK WOMAN, published by Wm. Morrow & Co., 1970. Reprinted by permission of the author.

"Secrets": Reprinted with the permission of Charles Scribner's Sons, an imprint of Macmillan Publishing Company from MOURNING DOVES by Judy Troy. Copyright © 1993 Judy Troy. (Originally published in *The New Yorker*, August 31, 1992.)

"The Orphaned Swimming Pool": From MUSEUMS AND WOMEN AND OTHER STORIES by John Updike Reproduced by permission of Hamish Hamilton Ltd. and Alfred A. Knopf, Inc. Copyright © John Updike, 1970.

"The Sojourner": From THE BALLAD OF THE SAD CAFE AND COLLECTED SHORT STORIES by Carson McCullers. Copyright 1936, 1941, 1942, 1950, © 1955 by Carson McCullers. Copyright © renewed 1979 by Floria V. Lasky. Reprinted by permission of Houghton Mifflin Co. All rights reserved.